MOTHERS
—and—
DAUGHTERS

MENDING A STRAINED RELATIONSHIP

TEENA M. STEW

BEACON HILL PRESS
OF KANSAS CITY

Copyright 2012
by Teena M. Stewart and Beacon Hill Press of Kansas City

ISBN 978-0-8341-2836-1

Printed in the
United States of America

Cover Design: Darlene Filley
Inside Design: Sharon R. Page

Library of Congress Cataloging-in-Publication Data

Stewart, Teena.
  Mothers and daughters : mending a strained relationship / Teena M. Stewart.
    p. cm.
  Includes bibliographical references (p.   ).
  ISBN 978-0-8341-2836-1 (pbk.)
  1. Mothers and daughters—Religious aspects,Christianity. I. Title.
  BV4529.18.S74.2012
  248.8'431—dc23

2012011674

10 9 8 7 6 5 4 3 2

To my mother, whose words and actions
still speak wholeheartedly of her love for me.

This work reflects the author's present recollections of her experiences over a period of years. She conducted numerous interviews with women regarding their mother-daughter relationships. Because of the sensitive nature of the content, certain names have been changed to maintain confidentiality.

Many thanks to the numerous women who were willing to share so openly about their relationships with their mothers.

CONTENTS

PROLOGUE

Several years ago after an exasperating phone call from my mother, I poured out my frustrations during my women's small-group meeting. I can't recall the exact details of the cause of my distress. I had most likely been subjected to a run-on "dialogue" and had listened at length to a string of negative complaints from my mother regarding her real or imagined illnesses or fears that the world was out to take advantage of her in some way.

I felt absolutely alone and miserable in my broken mother-daughter relationship. As I finished sharing my heartache with my small group, I was surprised to learn that several other women were experiencing similar struggles. I indeed had wondered, *Are there others as well?*

Following that meeting, I polled other women acquaintances, including some writer friends online, and found that many had strained relationships with their mothers. Their challenges range from controlling mothers who can't let go of the reins to deep-seated hurts caused by severe dysfunction.

Mothers and daughters have a unique bond. Fathers may love their daughters but will never know what it means to carry a child inside a womb for nine months, nor will they experience the excruciating pains of childbirth. Nor do most fathers understand the sacrifices mothers make in order to keep the children they bore safe and nourished.

Mothers love much—sometimes too much—unintentionally twisting their love into distorted "smother love." What daughter at one time or another hasn't felt the sting of well-intended motherly advice intended to protect and guide her? Too many of these negative encounters may cause us to promise ourselves that we will make every possible attempt never to be like our mothers.

Many women harbor matraphobia, the fear of growing up to be like one's mother. Despite that dread, many of us find ourselves walking in our mother's footsteps. We experience the same heart-tugging as our own mothers did when our daughter takes her first step, goes off to kindergarten, learns that Santa Claus isn't real, secures a driver's license, or eventually marries and starts her own family.

We do things we thought we would never do to try to protect our children from harm. We say things we never thought we would say, examining ourselves with astonishment as we realize that the motherly cliché we've just spouted came directly from the lips of our own mother. Suddenly we begin to understand. Mothering is hard, and it doesn't get any easier when our children move out on their own. Elizabeth Stone put it succinctly when she wrote, "Making a decision to have a child—it's momentous. It is to decide forever to have your heart go walking around outside your body."[1]

It is my hope that this book will bring a greater understanding between mothers and daughters, will tighten their bonds, will ease the chaffing—even if just the slightest amount—so that we move one step closer to heaven and farther from the difficult relationships many of us experience.

ONE
WINGS AGAINST A WINDOW

My mother and I have an understanding.
We've agreed not to understand each other.
—Renee Zellweger as Beatrix Potter in the movie *Miss Potter.*[1]

For nearly ten years my husband, my children, and I lived in Erie, Pennsylvania, in a 1920s two-story rough brick home with a full-size attic and a postage-stamp-sized backyard. Tightly nestled between two neighboring houses, it boasted a spacious front porch, which made up for its small yard. The porch was enticing, the kind made for sitting outside during raging thunderstorms and breathing in the musty scent of rain from the safety of a porch swing.

Our Erie home also had a detached two-and-a-half-car cinder-block garage. Near the peak of the garage roof were paned windows that allowed natural light to stream in. We often left the garage door open during the day so the kids could have easy access to their outdoor toys. Consequently, an occasional bird flew in. Fooled by the light from the windows, the creature would futilely beat its wings against the glass, unaware that freedom lay behind it.

At times while pining for and trying to duplicate good mother-daughter bonds, I have identified with those desperate birds beating frantically against a closed window. My wings have felt tattered, my emotions bruised. How I have longed to be a daughter who calls her mother for happy weekly chats or goes with her out to dinner or shopping excursions! Instead, when the phone rings and I see my mother's name on the caller ID, I dread answering. The relationship I share with her is not ideal. It is, however, improving and has moved from a work of destruction to a work of reconstruction.

THE TIE THAT BINDS ALSO GAGS

I never realized I had a poor relationship with my mother until my father died when he was fifty. We were very much alike; consequently, we were always close. We shared the same passion for reading and collecting books. We both had a strong creative streak and an aptitude for art. Dad was skilled with pencil and paper, and I remember with delight sitting in the attic looking through his old art books and sketches. He also loved to sing and play the harmonica. Music strengthened our tie.

In my mind I can still hear his rich baritone voice resonating through our church's small sanctuary as he sang in the men's quartet. In high school I, too, discovered my musical abilities and participated in concert choir, madrigals, girls' barbershop group, and an interdenominational Christian singing group called Remnant. The bond Dad and I shared was special.

My parents were both Depression-era children—practical and hard-working. They could squeeze a dollar out of a nickel. I endured countless lectures on running a minimal amount of bathwater in the tub and how to make do with only one paper towel. Nevertheless, despite his frugality, my father knew how to play.

It wasn't until I was a young married that I realized Mom didn't really play. I don't think she ever learned to enjoy life. For her, living equals drudgery and responsibility, an uphill battle in a dark and threatening world.

Just a few years after I married, my father succumbed to cancer after three years of treatment. Mom must have felt like a sailor clinging to the deck of a vessel that had run aground. Left to fend for herself and my youngest sister, Wendy, the only one of five siblings who still remained at home, Mom did the best she could.

In those early years of my marriage, my husband, Jeff, saw negativity surfacing in me, and he quickly pointed out this tendency of mine to look on the dark side. His words stung like alcohol on a scraped knee; yet I knew instinctively that his observations were true. Like many others, I was a product of my upbringing by a perfectionist father and a critical mother.

Proverbs 27:17 holds a wonderful truth: "Iron sharpens iron." Staying in close association with those whose actions and words smooth and hone our rough edges makes us a better person. Though I didn't particularly like the fact that Jeff had pointed out my shortcomings, I begrudgingly admitted to myself that he was right. Some changes in my attitude were in order. Over time, with practice, I was able to alter my outlook. I complained less and began to look more on the positive side of life. I owe much of this ongoing transition to my marriage partner.

Mom, on the other hand, lost her marriage partner, the primary person who could have inspired her to refine herself. With her protector gone, Mom's insecurities rose to the surface. She allowed fear to assume the throne of her life. Having suffered through a difficult childhood, and as an adult whose wall around her safe world had crumbled, she was battered and bruised. There was no one she could trust, no one to keep her safe.

I moved away from home when I married, and the geographical distance mirrored Mom's and my distance in our relationship. In those early years I battled homesickness. My phone calls home to Mom and Dad eased some of the misery. However, after Dad died, the phone calls changed. I still called to touch base but often hung up the phone more downcast and discouraged than I had been before initiating contact.

When I did call, I shared only surface issues. With no one to counterbalance her, Mom's negativity and worries about her own health became more dominant. Mom did most of the talking during those conversations. I hesitated to share anything of depth, fearing that I would be misunderstood or that what I said would be shared with other members of my extended family. I wanted to be friends with my mother but felt that our relationship was strained.

My three sisters had nearly the same issues with Mom. Many women can identify with my earlier illustration of the trapped birds. We batter against a window, hoping to find our way to the freedom of a close, loving relationship. Unfortunately, our own brokenness, and that of those with whom we desire a whole relationship, gets in the way. The tie that binds also cuts, gags, and smothers.

TATTERED LOVE

That fact that many women fear they will turn out to be like their mothers is an indicator that their relationships with their moms are not what they should be. Some still cling to the hope that some day the awkwardness they experience and the hurts they feel will subside enough to allow healthy interaction with the person they love. Others, after years of being hurt during attempts at connecting, have given up.

Personality differences, poor listening skills, control issues, mental illness, wounds caused by a painful upbringing or marriage, inability or unwillingness to forgive, and even substance addiction are just a few of the reasons contributing to these rifts.

It's easy to think that we are the only ones experiencing these problems, but the facts indicate a different truth. While working on this book I had the opportunity to speak to numerous women regarding their mother-daughter connections. Their pain is evident as they open their hearts. Below are just a few of their comments.

"Troubled mother-daughter relationships seem to be a universal problem. I believe one of the reasons is because mothers have been the controlling force in their small child's life, and as the child becomes an adult, mothers continue to try to control" (Margaret).

"My mom is a recovering alcoholic. We struggle. Even though she's in recovery and is now a Christian, we still butt heads like two goats fighting over a choice scrap" (Carrie).

"Due to all in the past she still hangs onto, she has an unforgiving spirit and bitterness. She makes my monthly visits a terrible ordeal for me" (Marie).

"My mother raised me and my four siblings after my alcoholic father left us. . . . She worked in a prison to support us. She could be the most creative (painted tempera portraits of Santa or the Easter Bunny at holidays on the windows) and supportive (encouraged all of us to honor grad status in high school, always attended our concerts, plays, art shows, and so on) person in the world. But when her depression took hold, she could turn into a shrieking lunatic and make us wish we had never been born. It has been a life-long mystery to know which mother I would get on any given day: Dr. Jekyll or Mr. Hyde" (Linda).

"My mom is very controlling and domineering, and our relationship is very shallow too. Basically, she talks and I listen—or pretend to. Now that she's gotten hard of hearing, she has an excuse for "poor listening skills" except that's the way it's been all my life. None of my adult children really like her" (Rachel).

"When I was a child, my mom was great. She was a stay-at-home mom, active with all our activities (I have one younger sister and younger brother) like Scouts, ballgames, fun home life with indoor and outdoor games, gardening, fishing, swimming. But when I was about eight or nine, my mother had to go to work full time, and that changed her relationship and her attitude toward us. Work became her focus, her passion—her kids and her husband, our dad, became her secondary life" (Beth).

GROANINGS WE CAN'T EXPRESS

As I listened to these women tell their stories, I saw the misery in their lives. They tried their best to express it in words, but in reality I could only partially understand the depth of their hurts. Their stories are, in a sense, written groanings.

When we go through difficult circumstances, we cannot always put into words—though we may try—the longings of our hearts or the pain we are experiencing. This is especially true in broken relationships. Brokenness makes us inwardly groan. It weighs down our spirit and extinguishes joy we might otherwise have.

When despair threatens to overtake us and we feel completely alone, it's important to remember that we are not. There is one closer than a brother, sister, or mother who treasures a loving relationship with us deeper than we will ever have with any spouse or human relation. The Holy Spirit is Comforter, Counselor, and Intercessor. He knows and feels our pain.

Jesus promised us when He left that He would send a Counselor in His place. In John 16:7 He said, "Very truly I tell you, it is for your good that I am going away. Unless I go away, the Advocate [Counselor] will not come to you; but if I go, I will send him to you."

The Counselor isn't meant for just anyone. He was specifically sent for those who choose to follow Christ. The Holy Spirit helps us be shining lights in a dark world. Jesus knew the wretched brokenness we would face in the world even in close places such as family relationships. If we are going to stand firm for Him, He wants us well-equipped to do so.

Romans 8:26 tells us, "In the same way, the Spirit helps us in our weakness. We do not know what we ought to pray for, but the Spirit himself intercedes for us with groans that words cannot express."

We may be locked into hurtful relationships we must deal with indefinitely. After days, years, and months of trying to cope, it can wear us down. When our situation appears hopeless with little chance for improvement, it is good to remember that there is another who not only can identify with our struggles but also feels our distress. He takes the pain on himself, just as one puts on a heavy garment.

DO YOU WANT TO BE HEALED?

God sees our distress and comes to our aid, but He won't provide assistance unless we are truly ready for it. The story of Jesus and Bartimaeus is a wonderful example of this. Jesus, surrounded by a large crowd, was preparing to leave the city of Jericho (Mark 10:46-52). As he passed by where Bartimaeus, a blind man, sat begging, Bartimaeus heard the noise of the crowd and asked another beggar what the excitement was about.

"It's the prophet, Jesus from Nazareth," replied the man, "the one who does great miracles." Bartimaeus tilted his head, straining to pick out Jesus' voice above the din of the mob.

He had heard of this man and the many miracles He had performed. His skin tingled from the excitement in the air. His one chance at healing was about to walk out the gate. Determined to gain Jesus' attention, he cried out in a booming voice—"Jesus, Son of David, have mercy on me!" Still fearful that his opportunity was passing him by and ignoring the rebukes to be quiet, he called out again.

Jesus stopped and looked around, and then His eyes fell on Bartimaeus. "What do you want from me?" Jesus noted Bartimaeus's hazy eyes and immediately knew why the man had called out. Still, He wanted Bartimaeus to express his desire for wholeness.

"Rabbi, I want to see." Only after he told Jesus that he wanted his sight did Jesus heal him.

Odd, isn't it, how Jesus often made those He chose to heal express their desire for healing aloud? Surely, as the son of God, He already knew and could see what the need was. Perhaps He knew that making the man state his request aloud helped him acknowledge what was broken within himself.

In our relationships we may know in our deep places that something is broken, but exactly what that is may not be fully known until we speak of it aloud. In the next few chapters you will embark on a healing journey to restore, as much as possible, your mother-daughter relationship. The Scriptures tell us that God heals the brokenhearted and binds up their wounds (Psalm 147:3). Many of us are walking around wounded. God wants to restore our relationships to wholeness.

The Bible contains many examples of reconciliation: Esau reconciled with Jacob (Genesis 33:4), Joseph with his brothers (Exodus 45:3-14), Christ with Peter (John 21:15-19), and the loving father with his prodigal son (Luke 15:11-31). If it can happen for them, it can happen for you.

Just as Bartimaeus wasn't brought to wholeness until he admitted his infirmity and desire for healing, we cannot experience healing and restoration until we first understand and acknowledge our need. The next step is allowing God to work in us to create the change we want to see.

HEALING THOUGHTS

1. As you read through this chapter, did you feel any kind of kinship with the women who shared their stories? If so, which ones? _____

_____

_____

2. Use descriptive words to define your relationship with your mother—*hostile, frustrating* . . . _____

_____

_____

_____

3. Would you say that your relationship with your mother is a work of destruction or a work of reconstruction? _____

_____

_____

_____

4. Are your wings tattered? Do you feel trapped while longing to break free? Use the space below to write a paragraph about your relationship with your mother. _____

_____

_____

_____

5. In Mark 10:46-52 we see that Jesus asked Bartimaeus what he wanted from Him. If Jesus passed by right now, what specific request would you make for healing? _____

_____

_____

_____

TWO

THE PERFECT RELATIONSHIP MYTH

"In some sense every parent does love their children,"
she responded, ignoring his second question.
"But some parents are too broken to love them well,
and others are barely able to love them at all."[1]
—Papa, in *The Shack*[1]

In the photograph actress Gwyneth Paltrow appears completely at ease. Eyes closed, dressed in an elegant white evening gown that accentuates her slender neck and upswept hair, she leans back against the comforting embrace of her mother, Blythe Danner. Both women are remarkably beautiful with facial similarities so alike that no one could mistake them for anything other than what they are—mother and daughter.

The photographer has crafted a beautiful portrait that emotes a sense of tranquility and security and something more—a surreal moment of an ideal existence between a mother and daughter. The two seem so at ease in one another's company that they need say nothing, just co-exist peacefully in the same space.

What woman hasn't longed for such a mother-daughter relationship? The carefully staged portrait of Gwyneth and Blythe, however, is just that—a staged portrait. The photographer painstakingly considered their wardrobe, the lighting, the backdrop, and the pose. None of it happened by chance. Though the younger actress may indeed have a good rapport with her mother, it is undoubtedly imperfect. Even if their bond is as close as the photo implies, at times their relationship may be pulled snug and taut like a comfortable pair of perfectly fitting jeans. At other times their bond may feel frayed, stretched, and dangerously thin.

On a daily basis we interface with human beings laden with idiosyncrasies and shortcomings spawned by unique upbringings. We even exhibit these ourselves. For better or for worse, our personal history forms us into who we are, and we are left trying to make relationships work despite these quirks. Close-knit friendships between mothers and daughters are a rarity. On occasions when we do glimpse what appears to be a healthy, tight relationship between a mother and daughter, we may view them through a filter, making their relationship appear perfect and more desirable than it actually is.

A FAIRY TALE FRIENDSHIP

Comfort, tenderness, love, and intense longing are the feelings I experience when I view the enchanting photo portrait of Gwyneth and Blythe. Like many women, I desire a fairy tale friendship like this with my own mom. I am not alone. Fascination with the romantic starts at an early age for many women.

I am reminded of Jaycee, a little redheaded girl at our church in California. Jaycee was enchanted with princesses. She had every imaginable related book and movie—*The Little Mermaid, Aladdin, Cinderella, Sleeping Beauty, Enchanted*—and the dolls, dress-up clothes, and toys to go with them. Her conversation and play time were filled with enchanted imaginings. In Jaycee's world fairy tales were very real.

Many women grow up with an idealized concept of relationship. As children, we were captivated by fairy tales of princesses and princes who fell in love, married, and lived happily ever after in a castle in a mystical kingdom. We desperately want the myth to be true even though common sense tells us it isn't. Even if we meet and marry our own Prince Charming, the marriage, even an excellent one, never matches the passion and perfection of a fairy tale romance.

Like Sleeping Beauty waking from a deep sleep, we may be stunned and hurt to learn that the person we love and thought was so perfect is human after all. At some point Prince Charming shows the chinks in his armor and tumbles from his horse. We learn about the fallibility of character and the work required in order to have a close liaison with someone we care about.

When reality hits, we either settle for less, working to make it better, or call it quits. We learn a new truth. Love relationships require work on both sides. Many women, however, still unwittingly cling to a fairy tale belief of perfect mother-daughter connections. We may carry expectations of what we want in our relationships with our mothers into adulthood. If we are able to adjust our notions in order to make our romantic relationships work, why do we have such a difficult time making allowances in our maternal relationships?

Perhaps it is because they are more deeply seeded. They go back to our roots. By the time we reach adulthood, we've already formed unhealthy ways of coping with the disparity between the love we know our parents possess for us and the imperfect way they showed it while raising us. We arrive clinging to a fairy tale because we desperately want to be perfectly and wholly loved. The desire, though imperfectly executed, springs from a holy source. God instilled in us the innate longing to both love and be loved. We are meant to reflect the relationships we can have with our Heavenly Father.

THE LONGING WE CANNOT EXPRESS

Deep in the heart of every person is a yearning for a loving, intimate relationship. If we are isolated from that companionship, we profoundly feel the loss. That's why a few days in solitary confinement can seem like an eternity to a prisoner.

We are designed for fellowship, and we mirror our Heavenly Father's nature—though we often fall miserably short. God, more than anything else, longs to be our closest companion. He wants intimate communion with us.

His every action proves this again and again—from the very beginning when He created Adam in His own image.

> Then God said, "Let us make man in our image, in our likeness, and let them rule over the fish of the sea and the birds of the air, over the livestock, over all the earth, and over all the creatures that move along the ground." So God created man in his own image, in the image of God he created him; male and female he created them *(Genesis 1:26-27)*.

Then He created Eve to fellowship with Adam (Genesis 2:18) so that He might not suffer the loneliness of isolation. "The Lord God said, 'It is not good for the man to be alone. I will make a helper suitable for him.'"

God's deep love for us is revealed throughout history. We are such simple, finite human beings, and God is so God-like—all-knowing, all-seeing, all-powerful—we can grasp only a fraction of what His nature is truly like. We see His love reflected in the way He cares for us, His children. In ancient times He provided a means for His chosen people to stay in fellowship with Him through sacrifice. "Make an altar of earth for me and sacrifice on it your burnt offerings and fellowship offerings, your sheep and goats and your cattle. Wherever I cause my name to be honored, I will come to you and bless you" (Exodus 20:24).

Without priests standing as buffers and intercessors on behalf of the people, they would never have been able to approach God. Despite the Ten Commandments, the guidelines God provided for the people, they kept breaking fellowship with Him. Finally he made the ultimate sacrifice for them. "For God so loved the world that he gave his one and only Son, that whoever believes in him shall not perish but have eternal life" (John 3:16). He sent His only Son to stand in the gap and be the sacrificial lamb so His communion with us could continue.

There is no greater love than the love God showed by allowing His only Son to be born as a frail mortal. Can you, as a mother, imagine the sole purpose of bearing a child being to sacrifice that child in order to save someone else? That's precisely what God did for us through His servant Mary. By giving Jesus up, God exemplified the ultimate in both fatherly and motherly love. What mother wouldn't lay down her life for her child?

Healthy, happy relationships—including those between mothers and daughters—are best drawn from this unselfish, non-condemning, longsuffering example of sacrificial love. Unfortunately, just like the Israelites, we fall so very short.

Only this Godly love, the love of Abba father (*av* in Hebrew, meaning "the one who gives strength") to the family[2] (*Ima*[3] [pronounced *ee-ma, em*] in Hebrew, meaning "the one that binds the family together"[4]) is the true and perfect model for us. It is this solidly stable love, a love that does not wound, that we will explore as we work through our relationships with our mothers. Much of what is covered can also serve as guidelines and insight into how to improve relationships with our daughters.

DIFFICULTY MAKING THE LONGING A REALITY

Like the artist or musician who has the image of a painting in his or her head or a song in his or her heart, when we try to put our creative imaginings on canvas or paper, we are often disappointed with the results. The reality never matches the imagined. Just as the picture of Gwyneth Paltrow and Blythe Danner stirs in us a longing for a bond like theirs, we may harbor in our hearts and minds a picture of the ideal mother. The gap between what we wish for and what we actually experience is the cause of much friction and distress.

When I started researching this book, I planned to share from books and movies that showed both idealized and healthy mother-daughter relationships, but my search revealed that there appear to be more negative examples than positive ones. Evidently book publishers and film producers feel that troubled relationships create conflict, making for more interesting stories.

One rare, positive example is found in the classic story by Louisa May Alcott's *Little Women*. Left to raise five daughters on her husband's meager salary while he was off fighting in the Civil War, Mrs. March proved to be a woman of courage and fortitude. At one point she spoke of her motherly desires for her daughters.

"I want my daughters to be beautiful, accomplished, and good; to be admired, loved, and respected; to have a happy youth; to be well and wisely married and to lead useful, pleasant lives with as little care and sorrow to try them as God sees fit to send."[5]

What mother doesn't want this for her daughter? Unfortunately, when maternal aspirations for daughters don't line up with a daughter's goals and desires, when their behavior doesn't align with their mother's, it can make for a miserable coexistence.

Consider the following broken relationships depicted in movies and books. Maybe you can relate to some of them.

Autumn Sonata, Ingrid Bergman's last film, cast her opposite her daughter Ingmar as a mother who forsook her family to pursue a music career.[6] Years later when she seeks to reconcile, her daughter voices a torrent of pent-up frustration.

In *Mermaids*, Winona Ryder and Christina Ricci star as two daughters doomed to frequent relocation because of their dysfunctional single mom's (played by Cher) flamboyant and flirtatious lifestyle.[7] Winona's character seeks equilibrium by becoming devout in her faith, while her mother seems bent on destroying any chance for her offspring's happiness.

Famous actress Joan Crawford unleashed a nightmarish world of skewed parental love on her adopted daughter Christina.[8] Christina tells of her twisted upbringing in her autobiographical book *Mommie Dearest*, which was later made into a movie starring Faye Dunaway. After viewing the movie one can only ask, *If this is mother-love, then what does hell look like?*

In *Because I Said So* Diane Keaton plays a controlling mother meddling in her daughter's love life as she tries to connect her with Mr. Right in order to prevent her daughter from making the same mistake she did.[9]

Christian writer Stephanie Whitson's book *Unbridled Dreams* features a teenage daughter who balks against her mother's confining plans to be schooled and refined as a proper young lady.[10] Instead, she runs away to pursue a future as a trick rider in Buffalo Bill's Wild West Show. The resentment and hurt both feel toward one another begin to heal only when they gain a deeper understanding of the motivations that guide their behavior. In the process they learn to forgive one another.

And finally, the last, my favorite, a book written several years ago by author Denise McGregor: *Mama Drama: Making Peace with the One Woman Who Can Push Your Buttons, Make You Cry and Drive You Crazy.*[11] I think that title pretty well sums up mother-daughter struggles. We have all at one time or another been a victim of "mama drama," and because of our less-than-perfect relationships we often create and aspire to idealized, unattainable standards.

PERFECTION VS. EXCELLENCE

Actor Michael J. Fox noted, "I am careful not to confuse excellence with perfection. Excellence, I can reach for; perfection is God's business."[12] When we create the "fairy tale" of perfect mother-relationships in our minds, we are sure to be disappointed, because they are based on perfectionism—and none of us is perfect. So when a relationship falls short, we are sorely disappointed and hurt.

Perfectionism is not what God desires for us, because it creates an unattainable standard. In their book *Leading Women Who Wound*, Sue Edwards and Kelly Mathews observe, "It's admirable to strive for excellence, but foolish to expect perfection.[13] Excellence pursues high standards but leaves room for mistakes and even expects them.

"The cost of perfectionism is that we are robbed of the satisfaction of a job well done. And we judge ourselves and everyone around us with an impossible standard that breeds discontent and dissatisfaction."

Lowering our expectations frees us to reach for something we have a hope of reaching. An excellent relationship allows for shortcomings and errors. In order to be a part of the friendships we aspire to in our relationship with our mothers, we must learn to mirror God's relationship with us. His sacrificial love provides a perfect model for us as we work toward a more meaningful, fulfilling relationship with our mother. This is the target we should aim for in our mother-daughter bonds.

IT'S GONNA TAKE A LOT OF TIME

I've attended several writers' conferences and in the process have met some interesting people. Only a handful of those who come to the seminars are top-selling authors. Others may have sold multiple books but never achieved fame of such magnitude. Still others may have a few publishing credits. Then there are the novices. Some, whom I call "writer wannabes," dream of being writers but have never written anything. Other newbies arrive, manuscript in hand, believing they have the next best-seller.

What typically happens with writer wannabes is that they are smitten by the dream of publication but don't have the work ethic to actually finish anything. The neophyte future novelist with the best-seller idea usually ends up either crying in his or her water glass at dinner or verbally bashing an editor because his or her work either wasn't what the publishing house was looking for or it wasn't polished enough for prime time.

The most successful writers are the ones who learn to make something positive out of the criticisms aimed at their writing and work hard at honing the craft. The hurry-up-and-get-there attitude that many novice writers exhibit also creeps into our relationships.

A few years ago singer Nicolette Larson's pop song "It's Gonna Take a Lot of Love" hit the charts. The lyrics talked about the time, effort, and love it was going to take to improve her relationship with a man she cared about. We live in an "instant society" that wants fast results and instant gratification. People hop from church to church with a consumer attitude, expecting churches to meet their felt needs but never really connecting and giving back. Many marriages—not all—end because it's easier to get a divorce than work through the tough spots. Even though it's still fully functional, we dump our existing technology—phone, iPod, PDA, computer—and replace it with something, flashier, faster, or better.

Sometimes this mind-set filters into our strained relationships. Like the novice writer who wants to be published without putting in the time to learn the craft, we may dream of an idealized mother-daughter friendship without working to make a better relationship a reality.

A FAIRY TALE FRIENDSHIP

A few years ago Mel Gibson and Helen Hunt starred in the comedy *What Women Want*. Gibson's character experienced a freak accident resulting in a severe electrical shock that left him with the ability to read women's minds. As you can imagine, it produced some hilarious results. If we were able to crawl into the minds of women and ask them what they want in their relationships with their mothers, what would they say? Here are just a few "wishes" women I talked to expressed:

Love. More than anything, we want to feel the love. Though we may believe our mother loves us, we may feel like a drought-shriveled flower because we don't experience it in the way she treats us or communicates with us.

Good communication. We want a mother who will listen to what we have to say without having to force ourselves into the conversation or without being interrupted. We want her to talk to us if something has hurt her rather than stuffing her emotions and giving us the cold shoulder.

Understanding and acceptance. We want the freedom to be ourselves without having to bear her disapproval, lack of response, or misinterpretation.

Trust and truth. We want to be able to believe what our mother tells us. Is she being straightforward, or is she attempting to manipulate us? Can we trust her to keep confidences and to be honest with us? Can we tell her the truth about what is going on in our lives without opening a floodgate of criticism, worry, or worse?

Self-awareness. We want our mother to be aware of her own shortcomings and idiosyncrasies rather than being oblivious to them.

Forgiveness. We are not perfect and inevitably make mistakes, but when we do, we want our mother to forgive us rather than hold them against us. When it comes to her own faults, even if she is aware of them, is she willing to admit she's in error and ask for forgiveness?

Solid, long-lasting friendships, even those between mothers and daughters, develop over time, and the key elements mentioned above are at the heart of their existence. Think of your own friendships, especially the deep ones. At some point in your friendship you've probably seen the fault lines in your friend's character. Maybe your friend talks too much or has pride issues. You may even have had spats or disagreements. It happens, but in most cases friends care enough to work through those differences, forgiving each other and delving into new depths in the relationship as they work things through.

This kind of closeness is not built overnight. It comes from persistence and trust. One person does not make all the necessary concessions in order for the relationship to work. It's tempting to look at the other person's deficiencies and expect him or her to change. In order to be friends with our mothers, we must first learn to model God's relationship with us. His love for us is both all-consuming and sacrificial, a perfect model for us to follow as we work toward a more meaningful and fulfilling relationship with our mother.

We read in 1 John 4:16, "We know and rely on the love God has for us. God is love. Whoever lives in love lives in God, and God in him." For many of us God remains an enigma. We cannot wrap our minds around Him. But this congeals His being into one word: *love*. God is love.

Now take the same verse and insert your name instead of God's. "_____ is love. Is it true? If you were to distill everything you are, would it boil down to love, the essence of God? A building is only as strong as its foundation. By establishing Christ, a portion of God's being, as our chief cornerstone (1 Peter 2:6) and role model, we create a solid structure on which we can build all relationships. When love is our foundation, how can we go wrong? Let's keep this important truth in mind as we begin to rebuild our relationships with our mothers, one stone at a time.

HEALING THOUGHTS

1. What are some of the improvements you long for in your relationship with your mother? _____

_____

_____

_____

2. Of the wish-list traits listed above, which do you feel needs the most work in your relationship with your mother?

_____

_____

3. Look again at the above traits. Where do you see areas you may personally need to work on? _____

_____

_____

_____

4. Can you think of examples that exemplify that God is love?

_____

_____

_____

5. Why do you think it is important for us to model ourselves after Christ in order to have good relationships? _____

_____

_____

_____

THREE

CULTIVATING FRIENDSHIP

*But Oh! The blessing it is to have a friend to whom one
can speak fearless on any subject; with whom one's deepest
as well as one's most foolish thoughts come out simply and
safely. Oh, the comfort—the inexpressible comfort of feeling
safe with a person—having neither to weigh thoughts nor
measure words, but pouring them all right out, just as they
are, chaff and grain together; certain that a faithful hand
will take and sift them, keep what is worth keeping, and
then with the breath of kindness blow the rest away.*
—Dinah Maria Mulock Craik[1]

Michelle Trachtenberg stars in the movie *Ice Princess* as Casey, a gifted high school student with an aptitude for physics. Casey's excellent grades place her on the scholarship path to Harvard University, her academic mother's (Joan Cusack) dream come true for her. In order to be considered, Casey must complete a physics project.[2] Urged to make it personal by her physics teacher, Casey arrives at the idea of interviewing and filming local area competitive ice skaters who will show the application of physics on a practical level.

Casey has always loved to ice skate but has no formal training. Taking her teacher's words to heart, she decides to film herself skating in the video as well. When she sees the video footage of herself, however, she's ashamed of her clumsiness on the ice. She decides to take a few lessons, and in the process she and her coach realize that with training she has the raw talent to become a champion. The passion she's always had for ice skating ignites, and Casey realizes that ice skating, more than anything else, is what she wants to do with her life.

Aware that her decision will upset her mother, Casey hides it from her for as long as possible. She clandestinely takes lessons but eventually faces the inevitable and goes head-to-head with her mother, who sees skating as a frivolous waste.

One of the more memorable moments in the movie is when the truth is finally out in the open and Cusack spouts, "You can't do this, Case. You're giving up your dream."

"No, Mom," replies Casey. "I'm giving up *your* dream. I'm going after *mine*."

Many women like Casey experience disharmony with their mothers when trying to break away from their control and make a life of their own. As young girls, we depend on our mothers for guidance and advice, which ensures our well-being and prepares us for independence. As we mature, parenting should transition from control toward guidance and then, as we get into our late teens and early twenties, to mentoring and friendship.

Unfortunately, all too often this isn't what happens. Discord occurs when mothers continue to view daughters as children and have difficulty letting go of control.

Women sometimes mourn choices they have made that they can't do over. This is one of the reasons mothers try to control their daughters. Just as Casey's mom wanted Casey to attend prestigious Harvard University and have the education she had dreamed of for herself, moms often aspire to give their daughters the life they personally could never have.

Some mothers try to fill a void in their own lives by living vicariously through their daughters. We'll delve deeper into control concerns and void validation in subsequent chapters. When our relationships are this skewed, it's hard for us to imagine a congenial interface with our moms.

As surprising as it may seem, however, many women are actually friends with their mothers. Such friendships don't happen by accident but are built brick by brick.

THE FRIEND WE WISH WE HAD

Susan talks with her mother, Anna, several times a week, and though they live several states away from each other and see each other only a couple times a year, they remain close. The two artistically inclined women share a love of literature and chic flicks, enjoy swapping recipes and discussing their latest craft projects. Susan is comfortable sharing deep things with her mother, because she knows Anna will lend an understanding ear without judging her.

Anna has deliberately cultivated this friendship with her daughter because she missed having such a bond with her own mother. Anna and Susan have successfully made the shift from parental control to parental mentoring and friendship. Some women have always held a close-knit friendship with their mothers, while others have learned to make adjustments in order to have such a relationship. Here is what a few have to say about how they and they mothers get along:

We have dinner at least once a week. We go shopping whenever I can find the time, and we have a lot of church activities together. Occasionally we'll go out to lunch or something, and we chat on the phone every other day or so (Roseanna).

My mother and I are so much more than mother and daughter. We are friends, calling to chat, exchange ideas, and she is my biggest fan of my writing. More than blood connects us. We are kindred spirits (Cynthia).

Mom knows she can talk to me without the chance I will repeat what is said to anyone else in the family. Trust is a huge factor. Mom also comes to me now for advice on spiritual matters or how to deal with some of the issues in our family (Allison).

Our relationship is great in part because my mom invested so much in me as a child and young adult. She home-schooled us and worked on the relationship and training me to be an adult— even when as a teenager I didn't appreciate her stance. But once I started college, our relationship quickly transitioned to friendship. I remember as a young teenager laughing when many of my friends told me their mom was their best friend. I couldn't imagine that occurring with us. Now, I can honestly say she is. She is always available to talk, give counsel and wisdom, or just listen. But it's also a two-way street. She also seeks advice and counsel from me. And we both challenge each other in our faith. I love that I can pull on her years of experience and wisdom, and yet she never forces it down my throat either (Cara).

The wonderful thing about my mom's and my relationship is that we can do anything, absolutely anything, and have fun doing it. We just finished painting the exterior of our house by hand with three-inch paintbrushes, and she kept commenting on how fun it was to work together. We like going out to eat, playing cards, plotting the books we write together, going to the symphony, going to the beach (Christina).

Mom was a lot older than most when I was born, and she encouraged independence. When I was old enough to be out on my own, Mom made it a point to come and spend time with me—even a month at a time. Mom tried to do things with me that I enjoyed doing, and she also tried to teach me things she enjoyed doing (Laura).

FRIENDSHIP BUILDERS

A person often has many acquaintances and yet may count only a select few of them as good friends. Earlier I indicated that friendship is built brick by brick. Camaraderie happens over time as we get to know and appreciate the other person. Friendship becomes a sturdy wall we can count on for support; each brick in this wall has a unique function. Its components include trust, acceptance, loyalty, willingness to share likes and dislikes, good communication, listening without criticism or interruptions, self-awareness of our shortcomings and idiosyncrasies, forgiveness, and sacrifice.

The stronger the components and the more of them two people share, the stronger the friendship. We don't necessarily have to be exactly like the other person in order to be friends. But we do have to like the other person, allow for differences, and find common denominators to make the relationship work. The stories of Jonathan and David and Ruth and Naomi provide biblical examples of deep friendship.

The first mention of Jonathan is on the battlefield just after David's incredible defeat of the Philistine giant Goliath. Jonathan no doubt witnessed Goliath's remarkable demise at the hands of David with only a sling and five smooth stones. After Goliath's defeat, when King Saul called David over to learn more about him, David was still holding the dead warrior's head in his hand (1 Samuel 17:57).

What a wild sight this ruddy-faced, short, muscular youth was to the king's son! He was immediately drawn to David's charismatic personality, and he admired both his bravery and strength of character.

Jonathan's spirit immediately bonded with David's. This was a relationship worth cultivating. "After David had finished talking with Saul, Jonathan became one in spirit with David, and he loved him as himself" (1 Samuel 18:1).

Ruth and Naomi's friendship wasn't as strikingly dramatic. The cords that bound Ruth and Naomi together through marriage grew closer as the years went by.

There was a famine in the land, and a man from Bethlehem in Judah, together with his wife and two sons, went to live for a while in the country of Moab. The man's name was Elimelech, his wife's name Naomi, and the names of his two sons were Mahlon and Killion. They were Ephrathites from Bethlehem, Judah. And they went to Moab and lived there.

Now Elimelech, Naomi's husband, died, and she was left with her two sons. They married Moabite women, one named Orpah and the other Ruth. After they had lived there about ten years, both Mahlon and Killion also died, and Naomi was left without her two sons and her husband *(Ruth 1:1-5)*.

Naomi's life had not been easy. In order to survive the famine in Naomi's native land of Judah, she, her husband, and their two sons moved from the people she knew and the town in which she had grown up to the land of Moab, where food was more plentiful. Moab was a foreign land with pagan beliefs. While there, Elimelech, Naomi's husband, died. She must have felt this loss keenly.

She did, however, have the consolation of her two sons, Mahlon and Killion, whom she could count on for support, and these young men married Moabite women, of which Ruth was one. Sadly, Naomi's hope for a happy future was quickly dashed. We are not told what happened, just that both young men tragically died, leaving all three women alone with no source of income. What a sad day when a mother outlives her husband and her children! Naomi's emotional wounds are apparent when upon her return to her native country she was greeted by acquaintances. "'Don't call me Naomi,' she told them. 'Call me Mara, because the Almighty has made my life very bitter'" (Ruth 1:20). In those days women relied on their husbands for their safekeeping, and with no one left to care for her or her widowed daughters-in-law, and no source of income, Naomi had no recourse but to go back to the land of Judah and throw herself at the mercy of her relatives there. She didn't know how she would feed herself, let alone Ruth and Orpah. So she did a noble thing and released them, ordering them to return to their own blood relations. Orpah complied, but Ruth would not hear of leaving her grieving mother-in-law.

But Ruth replied, "Don't urge me to leave you or to turn back from you. Where you go I will go, and where you stay I will stay. Your people will be my people and your God my God. Where you die I will die, and there I will be buried. May the

LORD deal with me, be it ever so severely, if anything but death separates you and me" *(Ruth 1:16-17).*

She was more than a daughter-in-law to Naomi. She loved her deeply. Ruth would do what she could to help Naomi, comforting her and accompanying her, even when it meant an unsure future and going to a foreign land where she might be ridiculed or even ostracized. Ruth and Naomi had moved from acquaintances to friendship. The two women respected and cared for each other.

David and Jonathan and Ruth and Naomi, comfortable in each other's company, were there for each other. They shared the laughs and good times and wept with each another when tragedy happened. Both friendships were tested and strengthened when Jonathan and Ruth were called on to assume a protective and sacrificial love for David and Naomi respectively. Jonathan put his own life at risk in order to protect David from his father, Saul. Ruth left behind her homeland and her relations to accompany her widowed mother-in-law back to Judah.

THE CRUCIAL COMPONENTS OF FRIENDSHIP

Let's look again at the crucial components of friendship and how those might apply to our mother-daughter connections.

Trust is the starting place, for it is the mortar that holds the wall of friendship together. It's so important that I'm devoting more space to discussing it than any other component. Without it, a friendship quickly crumbles. When it's present in a relationship, both know they can count on the other person when they need him or her, that he or she won't divulge confidences, and that the person will do what he or she promises to do. If trust isn't present, or if at best it is shaky, then the other person in the relationship may have difficulty trusting his or her companion and may either wish to cut him or her off, remain distant, or is willing to share only surface matters with him or her.

In my own relationship with my mom, I distanced myself from her because what I divulged in private either caused her to worry about me and my life choices or became public knowledge and was broadcast to my siblings, aunts, and uncles.

I also learned not to depend on her when she said she was coming for a visit. She has always been timid about traveling by herself to unfamiliar territory. The few times she did plan on visiting, she would say she was coming on a certain date and then in subsequent conversations give a variety of excuses as to why she might not be able to make it.

This played with my emotions, first making me hopeful, then dashing those hopes. In order to avoid further hurt, I emotionally distanced myself and learned not to expect her to follow through regarding visits.

Once trust is breached, it's difficult to regain it. You've probably heard the old adage about being twice burned. We may forgive someone for letting us down once or twice, but if he or she repeatedly lets us down, we determine we can't count on the person.

We all know that over time people can and do change. Whatever happened early in a relationship to break our trust may not be as likely to happen now. If we caused the breach, we won't quickly regain our mother's trust, but we can rebuild it over time, most likely through small gestures that show we are dependable. If, on the other hand, our mother caused the breach, we may be able to build trust by sharing small things with her as a test. Sometimes people mature as they age. She may already be aware of her past mistakes and need a second chance. A quiet, gentle, private talk might be in order to express the desire to establish trust and to share reasons why we struggle with it. This may open the door to laying this crucial foundation.

Acceptance is another component of friendship-building. Does our mother accept us for who we are, or does she try to change us to fit her mold? Do we accept her for who she is or wish she was different? There isn't much we can do if she has issues with who we are or how we live except to realize that when she criticizes us it is because she wants the best for us. When she has difficulty accepting us as we are, it indicates control or void validation issues. If on the other hand we have trouble accepting who she is, we are guilty of judging her, and this is not how God wants us to respond.

Jesus reminds us in Luke 6:37, "Do not judge, and you will not be judged. Do not condemn, and you will not be condemned. Forgive, and you will be forgiven."

Loyalty, another friendship component, guarantees that we are devoted to the other person and will remain steadfast and dependable for him or her.

Sharing likes and dislikes is the beginning of building trust. We can start simply, sharing small, surface-related matters, and then build to deeper layers. It helps to look for common ground. For instance, my mother, though not an avid gardener, does enjoy plants. I've learned to ask her advice on plants, and she has given not only shared knowledge but her plants as well. For special occasions I sometimes give her a plant or garden-related items.

Good communication is another very important element of friendship. Communication is more than just talking. It also involves listening and observing. Some researchers believe that communication is composed of up to eighty percent non-verbal communication.[3] Couples who have been married for a long time often know what the other is thinking or interpret each other's moods just by nonverbal cues.

This means there are many places where communication can break down and that how you communicate may not always be verbal. Someone's words and actions may mask his or her true feelings and motivations. Also keep in mind that if your mother is not a good listener, you may need to find better ways to convey your messages to her. For instance, if she doesn't stop talking long enough for you to say what needs to be said, you can either interrupt her to interject, or talk privately with her to discuss ways you can both work on making some changes so that you feel you are being heard.

Self-awareness, the ability to recognize one's faults and strengths, ensures that those in a relationship know their weaknesses and how they might annoy or hurt the other party. When there is low self-awareness, the chance for causing friction is much greater. Self-awareness is something we develop over time as people give us both positive and negative feedback. It should never be based on what one person says but rather on what a variety of people have said. If more than one person has made the same observation, it has more likelihood of being true.

We can increase our self-awareness by listening to and asking for feedback. If our mother is lacking self-awareness, we might gently point out things she does that annoy or hurt us without personally attacking her. Instead of using words such as "You know when you do such and such, it really hurts me," and instead say, "When such and such happens [notice we are not using "you" language], it really hurts me or makes me angry."

Forgiveness is a friendship factor. We must be willing to overlook the other person's idiosyncrasies and shortcomings and start afresh each time without holding it against the person.

Sacrifice is also a part of friendship. Friends care enough to give up something so that the other person benefits.

Remembering and practicing these friendship components can bring us closer to our mothers. It may require both cooperation and compromise.

Tamara found herself frequently at odds with her mother, a very opinionated and strong-willed woman who never backed down. When she disagreed with her mom, they frequently battled. It wasn't until Tamara learned to relinquish her need always to be "right" that she and her mother grew closer. She explains—

> As a daughter I make the sacrifice in not choosing subjects that will set her off into anger or resentment. She is an in-your-face woman. If I challenge her on any subject or disagree with her, she becomes resentful and angry. So I don't. It's worth it to me to have a relationship with my mother. It's not worth it to me always to be right.

Friendship means caring enough for the other person that we are willing to give up a part of ourselves in order to show our love for him or her. There's no better example of this sacrificial humility than God's friendship with us. He gave up His only Son and allowed Him to die in our place. "Greater love has no man than this, that a man lay down his life for his friends" (John 15:13).

Each time we work to make peace with our moms, even at the cost of dying to our own desires, we move a step closer to God-like nature and His ideal plan for us. If Jesus was willing to give up His life for us, shouldn't we be willing to make these small sacrifices for the sake of a relationship with our mothers?

HEALING THOUGHTS

1. Would you say that you and your mother are friends? What makes you think so? _____

_____

_____

2. Trust, acceptance, loyalty, sacrifice, similar likes, good communication, self-awareness, and forgiveness are all components that make up friendship. Choose one component you feel is the greatest weakness in your friendship wall with your mother. What can you do to strengthen it? _____

_____

_____

_____

3. What friendship component is strongest in the relationship between you and your mother? _____

_____

_____

_____

4. What can we learn from the friendship of Ruth and Naomi?

_____

_____

_____

5. Do you agree or disagree with the statement that we need to make sacrifices on our mother's behalf in order to become better friends with her? Explain your answer. _____

_____

_____

FOUR

FRIENDSHIP BARRIERS

*Mothers—and Fathers for that matter—
want what is best for their children, and sometimes
they have a very weird way of showing it.*
—Latest Dud[1]

Cori's conservative and controlling Christian mother, Marilyn, chose to home-school her three children because she desperately wanted to protect them from a hostile, non-Christian world. Marilyn screened their television shows, books, and friendships, making sure they watched or read only Christian material and associated solely with Christian friends.

She objected to the way some moms gave into their children's demands for designer label clothes—many of which she felt were immodest. When her children needed new clothes, Marilyn left them at home with their dad while she shopped for the items herself. Though the clothes weren't what the kids would have chosen for themselves, the children knew better than to question their mother's judgment and style choices.

Marilyn worked as a faux painter for an interior designer, and as a surprise gift to her daughter, Cori, and Cori's younger brother, while they were away at church camp, Marilyn repainted their rooms. Though Marilyn's intentions were admirable, because she had acted without consulting her daughter first, Cori saw it as a control issue and invasion of her personal space.

Marilyn also kept tight reins on her children in other ways, choosing which extracurricular activities they became involved in. Too bad if Cori hated piano lessons or softball, activities for which she had little aptitude or interest. If it was something her mom wanted for her, she had no choice in the matter.

By the time Cori entered her teenage years, she had had enough of "smother love." She and her mother frequently had heated battles, which usually ended in shouting matches. Cori sluffed off her school work, began smoking, and often lied to her mom about where she was going so she could spend time with friends her mother didn't approve of.

The tension didn't ease until Cori went away to Christian college—a college Cori had no say in choosing. She had wanted to attend art school. On the bright side, at least it provided a reprieve from her mother's controlling ways.

After graduating with her degree, Cori took a job in the same town as the college she had attended. Her mother, who had wanted Cori to live near her, was greatly disappointed. Nowadays Cori usually ignores calls from her mom, because she knows she'll ply her with questions about her life, voicing disapproval about her job, friends, and lifestyle. Deep inside, Cori loves her mother, but if she wants peace of mind, she needs to keep a physical distance between herself and her mom.

In chapter 3 we briefly touched on factors that stand in the way of mothers and daughters developing friendships with one another. The two most prominent are control issues and void validation. Cori's mom is an example of how a mother with control issues may try to guide or force her daughter to perform or behave in a manner deemed acceptable to her. Her goal may be admirable—to protect her daughter—or she may unknowingly be living her life through her daughter because of an unfulfilled void in her own life. The problem of meddling mothers is centuries old. Several examples are found in the Bible.

Rebekah favored her son Jacob over his twin brother, Esau, and devised a scheme to deceive their father, Isaac, and cheat Esau out of his birthright:

> Look, I overheard your father say to your brother, Esau, "Bring me some game and prepare me some tasty food to eat, so that I may give you my blessing in the presence of the Lord before I die." Now, my son, listen carefully and do what I tell you: Go out to the flock and bring me two choice young goats, so I can prepare some tasty food for your father, just the way he likes it. Then take it to your father to eat, so that he may give you his blessing before he dies *(Genesis 27:6-10).*

Rebekah's plot worked. Esau traded his birthright for a bowl of stew, and Rebekah and Jacob completed the plan by disguising Jacob as Esau, deceiving Isaac into giving Jacob his blessing. When Esau realized what had transpired, he threatened to kill Jacob, who fled for his life. Thanks to Rebekah's meddling, the birthright she had so elaborately schemed to secure was virtually valueless, because Jacob could not "redeem it" for his father's holdings. Instead, he had to make his living from scratch in a foreign land.

Had Rebekah realized the rift she would create in her family and that her actions would send her beloved youngest son away from her loving embrace for many years, she might have rethought her plan.

The same can be said of the mother of Zebedee's sons whose aspirations for her children moved her to ask Jesus for special favors: "Grant that one of these two sons of mine may sit at your right and the other at your left in your kingdom" (Matthew 20:21).

Had she known His kingdom was not an earthly one and that a road of suffering and martyrdom lay ahead for Him and His disciples, she would never have asked such a question.

Like most mothers, she wanted what was best for her children. Unfortunately, what we think is best for our children and what truly is good for them may be two different things. Jesus said in Matthew 7:9-11, "Which of you, if his son asks for bread, will give him a stone? Or if he asks for a fish, will give him a snake? If you, then, though you are evil, know how to give good gifts to your children, how much more will your Father in heaven give good gifts to those who ask him!"

Parents want to oversee their children's well-being by giving them good opportunities, but their imperfect nature sometimes prevents them from knowing what indeed is best for them. If they possessed their Heavenly Father's perfect perspective as they guide and mold their children's lives, the outcome would be much healthier.

THE HEAVY BAGGAGE OF VOID VALIDATION

When my middle daughter began driving, my husband, Jeff, purchased hubcaps in bulk—I'm not kidding—because she constantly misjudged curbs and was always either damaging hubcaps or loosing them. Inexperienced drivers can do some pretty comical things. All jesting aside, though, turning a teen loose to drive after he or she earns his or her driver's license can be pretty nerve-wracking. I'm glad those days are over for us. We seasoned drivers understand the importance of defensive driving, while our children may not. They may not watch for people running red lights, or they may use poor judgment when changing lanes. If they're truly going to learn to drive on their own, we have to give them the freedom to do so—even if it costs a fortune in hubcaps.

Keeping our children safe and secure is at the core of healthy mothering. One of the best ways to do this is to control and curb our children's behaviors. In a healthy relationship, parental control loosens as a daughter ages, and we allow her to make her own choices. The older she gets, the more lightly we hold the reins until finally, by the time she moves out on her own, we are acting more as an advisor than a controller.

Ideally, this is how it should happen. Unfortunately, some women are never able to loosen their grip on their daughters—as we can see even in some biblical examples. As one person astutely put it, control is a way of retying the umbilical cord. A grown woman who remains tethered to her mother often grows to resent her attempts at control.

There are many ways to control. Some moms merely voice their disapproval if a child's choices are different from what they would have chosen. Others may be accomplished actresses, feigning hurt when their child goes against their desires. Still others may withhold praise, giving approval only when they feel their daughter has measured up to the standard they've set for acceptable behavior.

Concern for a child's well-being is one reason women seek to control their child, but another reason goes deeper than that. Many women are unaware that the trouble spots that create hang-ups with their children and spouse come from an empty place inside themselves. When something is missing, a woman may try to fill the void without even being aware of what she is doing.

Some mothers who have set aside their own goals and ambitions in order to raise a family may lose their sense of self in the process. They become a mere extension of their husband or children. As their children become independent, these moms may be faced with an empty life, because their identity is based on caring for people who may no longer need caregiving.

In other cases a mother may pin her dreams and aspirations on her daughter. If she notices her child has musical abilities, and she enjoyed being in chorus at high school, she may expect her daughter to do the same. I experienced this with my two daughters, who are very different from each other.

Gaby, my second oldest, felt the keen sting of sibling rivalry. More than anything, she hated living in her older sister, Rachel's, shadow. Charismatic, charming Rachel had landed lead parts in her high school musical and plays, while Gabrielle had always shied away from music and drama. However, when Gaby tried out and landed the lead part of the gum-chewing, bratty Violet Beauregard in our local community theater musical production of *Willie Wonka*, Jeff and I were both surprised and delighted. She projected her lines and belted out her songs in front of the live audience with confidence, exhibiting a natural theatrical ability that Rachel did not possess.

Though I participated in select singing groups in high school, I never had the courage to try out for any musicals or plays. When I saw Gaby's raw talent, I attached my unfulfilled aspirations to her and wanted her to do what I had not. The more I pressed her to try out for chorus, show choir, or drama at school, the more she balked, determined not to be compared to her sister. It frustrated me to see her "waste" perfectly good talent, but I finally backed off and allowed her to make her own choices. Had I continued to force my will on hers, it would have caused serious damage to our relationship.

I can now understand how many stage mothers try to live their dreams through their children. No wonder there are so many horror stories of child actors who grew into miserable adulthood. Once they finally break free of overbearing parental controls, many misuse their newfound freedom. We read about their exploits in the newspapers. That's not to say that all child actors are forced into acting against their will. I know of many whose parents were supportive because they knew it was their child's passion and not their own.

"Void validation" isn't always about control. Sometimes it springs from a mother making up for things she missed out on in her own childhood or marriage. Yvonne Joan Hill believes some of the conflict she experienced with her mother, Lily, can be traced back to her mother's unhappy childhood. When only twelve years old, Lily had been helping her mother take the Thanksgiving turkey out of the oven when Lily's mother suddenly collapsed and died from a deadly stroke.

Lily's father was an alcoholic, and at the time of her mother's death, her older siblings were typical teenagers, too wrapped up in their own worlds to see the loneliness and heartbreak of a grieving twelve-year-old girl. With no one to coach or mentor her and no one to befriend her, Lily learned how to act and dress through innuendos and guesswork.

She was only nineteen when she married, and her need for nurture accompanied her into her new marriage relationship. Starved for affection she had never had while growing up, Lily, at times seeing the affection her husband gave Yvonne, competed against her daughter for his love. For a brief while as Yvonne entered young adulthood, Lily even mimicked how Yvonne dressed, wearing the same type of career clothes.

When Yvonne's dad died suddenly, her mother transferred her needs to her. It wasn't until years later during a session with a family counselor that Yvonne realized her role with her mother was actually reversed. Yvonne in many ways had acted as her mother's caregiver. Lily had undoubtedly suffered from void validation.

For some daughters the mother-daughter friendship they could have becomes skewed because of a lack of nurture or affirmation when their mother was younger. Such was the case with Kathy's mother. "She always expected me to be her companion, chasing other friends away in her life and mine. I had to break away in my early twenties, with the help of friends and my husband, to establish boundaries."

Kathy's mother harbored a void validation that resulted in smother love. The greater the void, the more pronounced the dysfunction tends to be, and the less likely a mother and daughter will have a good relationship.

WHEN BASIC NEEDS AREN'T MET

A study by Manfred-Max Neef reveals that humans have nine basic needs: subsistence (food, shelter, work, physical and mental health), protection, affection, understanding, participation (responsibilities, duties, work, rights) recreation (leisure), creation (abilities, skills, work, techniques), identity (sense of belonging, self-esteem, consistency), and freedom.[2]

When these needs are not met, people may act out to fill the void. This is often what causes the hurts, conflict, and dysfunction in relationships. One of the goals of this book is to help each of us gain a better understanding of why our mothers act the way they do. When we understand more about their voids and ours, we respond more compassionately while realizing what needs are not being met. We may even learn how to fill those needs in a healthier manner.

One of the most poignant biblical examples of void validation is found in the story of the woman at the well in John 1-30. Something in the woman's past prevented her from being able to have a steady, healthy relationship with a man. By the time Jesus met her, she had had five husbands and was living with yet another man out of wedlock. We can only guess what had happened to her in her formative years to create such dysfunction and what caused the breakup of so many marriages. She may have been clingy, needy, or very controlling. Whatever the case, Jesus saw deep into her soul and touched her "empty places." Like so many women, she had been trying to fill a void with the wrong thing. Jesus was what she needed the most.

Penny can relate to the Samaritan woman's brokenness. A difficult childhood had created voids in her life. Her pastor father's meager salary didn't cover their family's living expenses, so her mother had to work full time. Tragically, Penny was repeatedly sexually molested in the home of one of her babysitters. It has taken her years to forgive her mother for what Penny perceived as a form of abandonment on the part of her mother, although she realizes now her parents were doing the best they could. But the frustration and isolation that resulted due to this horrific act created a longing for the love and acceptance that she never received while growing up:

I always wanted people to fill up the empty places in my heart and life. The empty places got bigger when I went through the abuse. I keep trying to push people into those holes in my life— trusting them to protect me, heal me, fix me, make me happy. But it wasn't until I started depending on God to do those things that I started to heal. He cleared my vision, and that paved the way back for my relationship with my mom to heal.

Penny's painful upbringing made her seek people to fill the voids in her own life. It stands to reason, the deeper the void, the greater the desperation to fill the hole. Such neediness can drive wedges between mother and daughter. Recognizing the causes of void validation and control issues helps us gain understanding and wisdom regarding how to respond to them and take measures to adjust our own behavior so we don't fall into the same trap. But what happens when controlling mothers remain out of control despite our increased awareness and attempts to make changes for the better?

CUTTING THE CORD

"Children, obey your parents in everything, for this pleases the Lord," Paul writes in Colossians 3:20. The Scriptures tell us to obey and respect our parents. Doing so results in two things: first, it pleases God. Second, it protects parents and their children from out-of-control behavior that can lead to disaster and distress if left unchecked. Despite this commandment, when we reach adulthood we are no longer expected to be under parental authority. While we are children, God sits in authority over our parents, who in turn serve in authority over us. As adults, we are no longer subject to parental authority, because God is then our acting parent.

He still wants us to respect our parents, but we are no longer under obligation to obey them, especially since we are starting our own households and families. When two groups of parents, you and your mother, are vying for authority over one household—yours—conflict is sure to arise.

If our mother has retied the umbilical cord, we may have to snip it. We do this by setting firm boundaries to distance ourselves from her control and gain the authority we lack over our own household.

One young woman who had recently moved out on her own reached her breaking point with her mother. Her mother called constantly, badgering her about whom she was dating, where she was living, where she was working, and the choices she was making. Nothing ever pleased her. Finally the daughter had had enough. Each time her mother started in on the attack, her daughter responded with "Mom, I love you, but that subject is off limits." After multiple responses like this, her mother saw that she had no control over her daughter and backed down. This savvy daughter didn't stop there. She knew her mother still needed to give advice, so she began seeking her mom's opinion in small things, even when she didn't really need the advice. By not allowing her mother to gain a foothold, she was able to regain peace of mind and still allow her mother to feel loved.

Simple changes are not always enough to curb control issues. Sometimes it takes a sizable sacrifice on our part to gain peace of mind. A daughter whose meddling mother lived nearby grew tired of her mother's verbal attacks against her spouse and their parenting choices. Her mother frequently dropped in unannounced, and her interference was causing serious marital strain. Though the couple loved where they were living, they knew they had to put some physical distance between themselves and Mom. They sold their home and relocated their family to a different city. Though it was an extreme measure, it was necessary for their own survival, and the peace of mind was well worth it.

Just as God had compassion and mercy on the Hebrew nation because of those who were causing them to bow under oppression, He has pity on those under the heavy burden of control. Isaiah 51:21-22 reads,

> Therefore hear this, you afflicted one, made drunk, but not with wine. This is what your Sovereign LORD says, your God, who defends his people: "See, I have taken out of your hand the cup that made you stagger; from that cup, the goblet of my wrath, you will never drink again. I will put it into the hands of your tormentors, who said to you, 'Fall prostrate that we may walk over you.' And you made your back like the ground, like a street to be walked over."

We are not to be doormats or puppets. When other people control us, even when doing it out of love, it becomes a form of bondage. God wants to help us break free of chains that keep us captive. When we allow others to control us in order that they might selfishly fulfill their own emptiness, we place ourselves back under bondage and essentially live a lie that says we must place their happiness above all else. This is rubbish.

Linda has struggled with her controlling mother all of her life. Though she has several siblings, care for her mother falls mostly on her since she lives the closest.

> Pray and honor what you can, when you can. You cannot put your life, your marriage, or your sanity in jeopardy for the sake of a relationship. Set strong boundaries, and have an escape plan, but keep trying. . . . My husband and I have her at our house every weekend, because she has no other social outlet. It is stressful, to be sure, but I tell myself it is not forever. I do not want regrets once she's gone. If she cannot abide by simple rules of our house, such as respecting our parenting and my husband's authority, she must go home early. My siblings visit and call when they can and help in other ways that we cannot, such as helping her financially. She will never be easy to get along with, but we continue to try.

Control issues and void validation produce lopsided relationships. Understanding why our mothers control or try to live their lives through us helps us recognize destructive patterns in our relationships with our own children and take measures to curtail them. Though God longs for restoration, He doesn't want us locked into a miserable existence just to keep someone else happy. Feeding someone else's self-indulgence and codependency does nothing to help him or her mature and heal.

When "smother love" threatens to take you down, seek God for solutions. Ask Him to reveal the barriers that stand between you and your mother and show you simple things you can do to lovingly address those issues while establishing healthy balance and boundaries. Knowing when to submit and when to take a stand is the beginning of healing.

HEALING THOUGHTS

1. Has your mother ever exhibited void validation? If so, give an example. _____

_____

_____

_____

2. Have you ever fallen into the trap of void validation with your own children? Give an example. _____

_____

_____

_____

3. Can you think of an instance in which a mother's attempt to control her child has caused serious negative consequences?

_____

_____

_____

4. Is there an issue in your relationship with your mother in which you need to take a stand? If so, what is it? _____

_____

_____

_____

5. Name one small thing you can do to break free of "smother love." _____

_____

_____

_____

FIVE

GETTING PERSONAL

*If we could read the secret history of our enemies,
we should find in each man's life sorrow and
suffering enough to disarm all hostility.*
—Henry Wadsworth Longfellow[1]

Every year on Jodie's birthday the same scenario played out when she unwrapped the gift her mother had given her.[2] Her mother would explain that she had purchased a bigger, better, or more extravagant gift than the one Jodie had just opened, intending to give it to her but had instead decided to keep it for herself. Once she had even purchased a coat for Jodie but had kept that as well. Several weeks later after wearing it a few times, she finally gave it to Jodie, claiming it was too big for her.

It didn't matter what the gift was—a purse, a hat, a scarf—Jodie's mother always behaved in the same odd way when giving her daughter gifts. She kept the best for herself and made sure Jodie knew it.

The mother's selfish behavior cut her daughter like a knife, and Jodie finally wrote to an advice columnist seeking insight. Why would a mother behave this way? Without having the full history, the columnist could only guess. She surmised that Jodie's mom was in essence telling Jodie that she—her mom—came first. Jodie's mom was trying to compensate for something inside her that was missing.

Who can say what caused Jodie's mother's strange behavior? Was she constantly denied love or material possessions when she was young? Without a knowledge of her history, it's difficult to say, but it would have surely helped Jodie understand her mom's hurtful behavior if she knew the motivating reasons for it.

As much as we think we are in control of our choices, behavior, and emotions in the present, our past often affects our behavior, and we may have to fight to change unhealthy or destructive patterns. We saw in the last chapter how many mothers over-compensate for some void in their lives. The emptiness or deficiency may go back to their formative years.

IS HISTORY DOOMED TO REPEAT ITSELF?

Have you ever stopped to consider your mother's upbringing? Take a moment to ponder her history now. As I have learned bits and pieces of my own mother's story, I have felt my heart soften toward her. Here is some of her story.

She was the youngest girl of thirteen children born to an alcoholic father who worked as a carpenter. I never met my grandfather, who died well before I was born, but I know the family was very poor, and Grandma Todd often had to get her husband's paycheck from him before he drank it away.

From some of the stories Mom told me, I know Grandpa Todd had a mean side, especially when he was drinking. He used a tree branch or a belt liberally to discipline his kids. He also used a gun to rid his property of unwanted cats. Mom also told me another horrific story about how she had accidentally killed a kitten. I'll spare you the gruesome details, but the horror still remained with my mother, who understandably had nothing good to say about cats when I informed her that Jeff and I had adopted a kitten.

Until my grandmother was in her seventies, the two-bedroom house in which my mother was raised had no indoor toilet or furnace. Can you imagine a two-bedroom house with thirteen kids? What I remember most about family reunions was that when my many aunts and uncles gathered en mass, everyone talked loudly at once and nonstop. As the youngest girl among that many siblings, my mother learned to talk, and talk she did, never taking a breath to let anyone else get a word in. In her household quiet people were ignored.

Just a few years ago I learned that my mother was held back twice in grade school. The rationale was that she was too immature. Knowing what I know now, I believe she has comprehension problems and may have an undiagnosed learning disability. All this history is something I learned in bits and pieces over time. I can't tell you how much it has helped me to develop a more forgiving spirit toward my mother. I suspect that one other reason for my mother's incessant talking is that it acts as a barrier that prevents people from being able to get to know her more deeply. I think she has a great fear that people won't like her, may even think she is dumb, if they know what she is really like. In many ways her behavior has become a self-fulfilling prophecy.

How well do you know your mother's history? Was there abuse? Was her relationship with her own mother a good one? Did she have unmet needs? Take a moment to write what you know of your mother's history, including the quality of relationships she had as a child—parental, friends, young adults.

Once you finish writing your mother's history, spend time recording your own history with your parents. What was good about it, and what was bad?

I'm in my fifties and have just begun to have a
meaningful relationship with my mother. Things
between us changed the most when God helped me to
see my mother as a woman—a person who got where she
is through her own life history—with scars, fears and
needs. It still grates on me when she starts in about
some problem member of the family, but now
I see her differently, and we've shared
some very special moments (Leslie).

The more deeply you know your mother, the more you can em-pathize with her behavior and choices. This knowledge will also provide you with wisdom when trying to cope with her sometimes frustrating behavior. Many components have made her the unique person she is today. As is the case in our own lives, we are often shaped by our environment and the people who raised us.

"All have sinned and fall short of the glory of God" (Romans 3:23). Not one of us is perfect. From generation to generation, de-spite their love for their children, broken parents and guardians guide and mold their children and often unintentionally pass along their broken methods of coping and thinking to their offspring, who in turn pass it on to their children.

Leviticus 26:39-42 illustrates that harmful behaviors and sinful actions can be transferred from one generation to the next. Though the words are spoken to the disobedient nation of Israel, they are still applicable to us.

> Those of you who are left will waste away in the lands of their enemies because of their sins; also because of their fathers' sins they will waste away. But if they will confess their sins and the sins of their fathers—their treachery against me and their hostility toward me, which made me hostile toward them so that I sent them into the land of their enemies—then when their un-circumcised hearts are humbled and they pay for their sin, I will remember my covenant with Jacob and my covenant with Isaac and my covenant with Abraham, and I will remember the land.

The brokenness imparted on us by parents with good inten-tions causes us to spiritually and emotionally waste away. If we are willing to admit the brokenness in ourselves and others and face it with contrite hearts, willing to forgive past hurts and wrongs, He is willing to forgive as well and allow for a fresh start.

Though we are forgiven, we may still have to battle demons in both our parents' and our own past. Through God's transform-ing grace, and with determination and hard work, we can overcome pains and heartaches caused by poor choices and dysfunction so that we don't pass on this brokenness to our children.

WHAT MAKES YOU WHO YOU ARE?

Without a doubt, our history shapes us, but there is another component that forms us as well. Our genes are like a frame that surrounds our personal portrait, and they have an important role in confining and defining who we are.

I have already shared about my two daughters, who are very different from each other. Both Rachel and Gaby are of average height, but they look nothing alike. Curly-haired Rachel inherited her broad shoulders and boxy build and, we suspect, her curly locks from the Stewart side of the family. Gaby has the Todd family's smaller bones, slender build, and straight hair. She eats anything she wants without gaining weight, has inherited my sensitivity to medication, and wrestles with depression, also a Todd trait. Rachel, on the other hand, has difficulty managing her weight but is nearly always cheerful.

Who we are depends not only on our choices and attitudes but also the traits and genetic makeup we inherit. Nature coupled with nurture shapes us. We are born with a unique personality, but we are also molded by the environment in which we are reared. Sometimes it is difficult for us to separate the two. Gaining insight into both our mother's personality and our own can help us know how she operates and what might cause us to be at odds with one another.

There are many different personality profiles that shed light on personality types. I will use the Enneagram of Personality[3] in this book, which I was first introduced to by a friend when I was struggling to complete a fiction novel. He suggested I use the tool as a way to more deeply develop my characters. By choosing personality types that were vastly different from each other, I could then create a scenario in which they would more likely be at odds with each other, thereby causing more conflict, which would make my story more interesting.

I was intrigued by the idea and read over the descriptions with interest. Enneagram describes the personalities and also diagrams them, assigning each a number and placing them strategically on a circle.

Each personality type has a unique set of traits that exemplify ways people think, feel, and behave. The idea is that the more we know about different personality types, the more effectively we can interact with one another. Understanding these unique trait sets can be beneficial for use in business, psychology, psychotherapy, career development, and countless other areas.

My purpose in introducing this resource is to give you a deeper understanding of your own personality as well as your mother's. Our makeup means we are more likely to get along well with certain personality types as opposed to others. The more clearly we see our methods for processing and responding and how those we associate with operate, the more we can improve while learning to understand how to interface with others. In the long run, this will result in fewer conflicts and misunderstandings. One important thing to remember is that most people have a prominent personality type and a few other personality types that also make up their nature.

Take a moment to look at the Enneagram of Personality in the Appendix. Try to identify your prominent personality type as well as the next two most prominent types you display. If after looking at them you are still not sure, ask some of your family members to help you decide which ones are most like you and which ones are most like your mother.

HOW IS YOUR MOTHER WIRED?

Now that you have an idea of your own personality type, look at the descriptions and determine which one best defines your mother. Now look at the diagram. Is your mother's personality next to or near your own, or is it extremely different, perhaps even on the opposite side of the circle? If so, the reason you and your mother have such a difficult relationship could be in part because you approach life and solve problems in radically different ways. Is that possible?

As the saying goes, knowing is half the battle. Understanding how you and your mother perceive and deal with life will also help you understand any conflict or distance between you. Some of this tension will ease when you change how you respond to her perspective and coping mechanisms.

While looking over the Enneagram of Personality descriptions, I was amazed to see my mother's personality so clearly defined. Suddenly the difficulties my siblings and I have experienced with her made perfect sense. My mother is clearly a number six on the Enneagram—a Loyalist——especially regarding the Loyalist's coping strategy. In a Loyalist's childhood the authority figure(s) who oversaw their care and discipline may have been unpredictable or untrustworthy. Consequently, the Loyalist may have learned to be on his or her guard in order to survive. Loyalists have a strong feeling of impending threat. They also have a complex relationship with authority figures. On one hand, they want those in authority to protect them. On the other hand, they don't trust them to do so.

My mother complains of every ache and pain and makes frequent trips to the doctor. However, if the doctor finds there is something wrong, Mom is usually not pleased with the way the doctor handled it. She distrusts the medical profession as a whole. If she receives a prescription, she's afraid it's the wrong one or that it won't be effective. If a medical expert gives her health care advice, she's skeptical of the diagnosis. The doctor is in a no-win situation.

Mom is equally distrustful of others, from the serviceman who repairs her gutters to the insurance agent she fears is out to take her money. The distrust runs deep and most likely goes back to a parent—remember her alcoholic father—who somehow broke her trust. After looking over the Enneagram of Personalities, I realized my mother's behavior is nothing personal—distrust is what she's always experienced.

When an earthly parent, guardian, or authority figure disappoints us as adults, the walls go up and the trust level goes down. When it happens while we are children, it raises even higher walls and creates an even deeper breach of trust. That mistrust may transfer to that person's perception of a heavenly parent. That's why many of us have difficulty believing that God is a just and loving God. We think He behaves in the same inconsistent way as our earthly parents.

Awareness of how you each operate can also help you avoid pushing one another's buttons. If you must talk with your mother about something and you can prepare ahead of time, ask yourself, *How would I normally bring this up?* Then ask yourself, *What is the best way to approach this without creating a misinterpretation or hurt feelings on her part?* You may still not be able to avoid conflict, but it may diffuse some of the volatility.

We've learned to respect and appreciate our differences. My mom and sister are social creatures, talkative and open. My dad and I are quiet, introspective, and happy to sit at home. Over the years we've learned that we can strike a balance—visit at home sometimes, go out sometimes. She respects my quiet sustainability, and I give her the chance to talk (Roseana).

ARE YOU SPEAKING A FOREIGN LANGUAGE?

We've often heard it said, "She and I don't even speak the same language," or "I'm not feeling the love." Have you ever felt that way in your mother-daughter relationship? So far we have delved into our mother's history, and we have pondered her personality. Both can help us draw closer to her. One additional thing we can do to help us "get" why our mothers act the way they do is to understand the "language" they speak.

It wasn't until a few years ago that I began to see that people express love in different ways. Sometimes our cultural heritage impacts how we cope with differences and show our affections as a family unit. For instance, I have a friend who is Italian. There is no guessing about how Liz feels. Her emotions are all up front. If someone does something to make her angry, she'll spew forth quite loudly, letting that person know exactly how she feels. Liz grew up in a home where family members yelled and screamed if they disagreed. It may not have been pretty, but no one hid their emotions.

My husband, Jeff, claims that his family, which is a mixture of German and English descent, handled disagreements in a similar fashion. "We loved each other at the top of our lungs." Jeff is also very physically demonstrative with his love and likes to give me hugs and kisses. He tells me frequently that he loves me. At times it must be like hugging an ice cube.

I came from a stoic family. I remember an incident that happened when I was a child of maybe eight or nine playing in the backyard. I don't fully recall the circumstances except that I was suddenly "filled with the spirit"—of childhood—and I let loose with a loud shout. I still vividly recall my dad turning to me and chastising me. "Quiet! Do you want the entire neighborhood to hear you?" I remember thinking *If I can't yell outside, where* can *I yell?*

Our family life was the same way. Emotions were squelched. The message that was silently conveyed was that if things became tough, we kept a stiff upper lip. It wasn't until I was an adult and the miles separated me from my mother and father that I remember hearing or even saying the words *I love you* to Dad. I never heard them from my mother.

Thank goodness, Jeff taught me how to hug. That isn't to say that my parents didn't love me. They did. They just didn't show it in a demonstrative fashion. Dr. Gary Chapman believes there are five love languages that humans use to convey their love to one another. Each of us has our own preferred method. Understanding these love languages can help us better understand how best to express our love to others and how to recognize they are showing love to us.

For years I was hurt by my mom's inability to show she loved me. All I got was criticism. I could not recall her hugging me, though I suppose it's possible she did when I was very small. Her frugal upbringing causes her to be uncomfortable buying gifts to show her love except around Christmas or for birthdays when it is expected, because to her, spending money for extras is wasteful. She has difficulty throwing away a broken spatula even if she is given a new one.

I can see now that she shows her love in different ways, and I am learning to translate the love language my mother speaks. Chapman breaks down the love languages as follows:

Quality Time. Some people feel most loved when those dearest to them take time out of their busy schedules to spend time with them. It's not so much how much time is spent but rather that time is set apart so that the recipient feels that he or she is front and center of the other party's affections. If this is your primary love language, and you don't receive this attention, you will feel unimportant and cast aside when these special "huddles" don't happen.

Quality time matters because it allows two people to get to know each other. It is a time for getting in touch with struggles, likes, and dislikes. As Chapman puts it, it is a time for self-revelation.

A task-oriented person will have a difficult time giving quality time to another, because it interferes with his or her ability to perform tasks. Performing tasks provides a sense of accomplishment and value. People who have trouble giving quality time are often those who were raised in households where time was considered valuable and where leisurely periods of time not producing something with a physically obvious outcome were considered wasted. My mom is one of these people, and this same task-oriented mode of operation is ingrained in me. I have had to work at spending quality time with my own children.

Receiving Gifts. Chapman believes gifts are symbols of love. For some of us, receiving and giving gifts comes from the deep places within us. I have a friend who speaks this love language. More than once I have received a small, unexpected gift from her. She delights in delighting others.

If this is your love language and you never receive gifts, or you feel little thought has been put into the ones you receive, you may not "feel the love" from the giver. Or if giving gifts brings you joy and the recipient brushes it aside or finds fault with it, it may cut you like a knife. My mother more often than not will find something wrong with a gift she receives.

For her birthday, my youngest sister and I agonized over what to buy her. We shopped at an outlet mall that was not in my mom's hometown and carefully thought our gift of clothing through. My mother is only five feet tall, so finding petite size clothing is imperative. We made sure before making our purchase to verify that the same clothing chain outlet was near her in case she needed to return anything.

It's a good thing we did, because, sure enough, what we chose was not suitable, and back to the store it went. My siblings and I have learned that receiving gifts is obviously not my mother's love language. After years of trying to please her with gifts, we have finally reached the conclusion that we would do better to buy a gift card, write a check, or take her out for a show or a meal.

Acts of Service. The primary love language for some involves doing something for someone. In a marriage a man might show he loves his wife by vacuuming the house, or a wife might take out the garbage for her husband. Acts of service are a form of servant leadership. The sacrifice of time and energy shows the other person that you put him or her above yourself.

It is important, however, to know what types of acts of service mean something to the other person and that they should be done out of love and not out of obligation. It has taken me years to realize this, but I believe that this may be my mother's primary love language, and she shows her love to me and my family by serving meals at family gatherings. When we come for a meal, she makes sure there is plenty of food. Acts of service, such as cooking for us, is one of her love languages—her way of nurturing her family and making certain she has adequately cared for us.

As a widow, it also touches her when we spend time with her and help with repairs or upkeep around the house. She gets to see us, and it makes her feel special. She seems to appreciate the sacrifice of time.

Physical Touch. We've already discussed how some people cherish physical touch and are comfortable with it while others may not be. If you love getting and giving hugs, this might very well be your primary love language. If you never receive this type of affirmation from your loved one, it can make you feel unappreciated and uncared for, and vice versa, if this is the love language the other party prefers.[4]

Just because you and your siblings grew up in the same household does not mean you, your siblings, and your parents have the same love language. Gaining a deeper understanding of what makes you and your mother feel loved can help you close the affection gap.

The Master of understanding people and the events that shape them is Jesus Christ. We see over and over in biblical accounts how He understands their past and both forgives and confronts them, urging them to change their behavior. There is a huge difference between trying to understand our mother's behavior and approving of it.

Understanding is the beginning of grace and compassion. If we want God to extend grace to us, we must learn to extend grace to others—including our mothers. Wouldn't we want the same done for us?

HEALING THOUGHTS

1. Does knowing your mother's history make you more tolerant of her quirks and methods of operating? _____

_____

_____

_____

2. Are there any changes you will make in your own childrearing, if applicable, in order to avoid some of the hurts your mother experienced in her formative years? _____

_____

_____

_____

3. Did you learn anything new about your mother's personality?

_____

_____

_____

4. When you compare your personality to your mother's, is there anything thing that might cause conflict between you?

_____

_____

_____

5. What changes do you need to make in order to speak your mother's love language? _____

_____

_____

SIX

HANDLING CONFLICT AND COMMUNICATION

❧

*The most important thing in communication
is to hear what isn't being said.*
—Peter Drucker[1]

When Sheridan was growing up, she longed to hear the words "I love you" from her perfectionist mom. Her mother frequently bragged to her about Sheridan's brothers and sisters but never spoke encouraging words to her. Years later, during a conversation with her sister, Tammi, Tammi revealed that their mother had often bragged on Sheridan to her. In that moment the two sisters realized that their mother had avoided praising them to their faces because she feared they might become conceited.

For years Sheridan had also been an aspiring writer, trying to work up the nerve to send her work out to publishers. Part of that struggle was caused by lack of self-esteem partially brought on her mother's lack of praise and encouragement and the constant barrage of criticisms and comparisons her mother leveled at her. Finally, after having several written pieces accepted, Sheridan took some of the published work to share with her mom. She held her breath and pulled out the copies.

Her mother quickly scanned the articles and muttered a couple of quick "hmms." Suddenly she rose out of her chair, went to a closet, and began rummaging through it. Soon she returned with a scrapbook. "Look!" she said, pushing it into Sheridan's hands. "I don't know why you've had such a hard time realizing you're a writer. You've always been a writer. I knew it years ago. That's why I saved this."

There on the left-hand page was a poem Sheridan had written in crayon and decorated with a red bird when she was in second grade. On the right-hand page was an award she had won for the poem after her teacher submitted it to a state competition. Her mother had cherished Sheridan's accomplishment with pride. Sheridan sat there with tears running down her face. Her mother had told her she loved her and was proud of her without using words.

Many of our mothers grew up in households where emotions were held in check. Consequently, outward shows of affection may have seemed inappropriate to them. Most mothers truly love their daughters, even though their love sometimes manifests itself in broken ways. When our mothers criticize or try to control us, we must learn to overlay a "love" filter to help us translate what they are trying to tell us. What our mother says, what we hear, and what she means may be three different things.

Proverbs 14:29 says, "A patient man has great understanding, but a quick-tempered man displays folly."

Sheridan's story provides an excellent example of how easy it is to misread what is actually being communicated. It is easy to lose patience when we feel we are misunderstood or under fire. The tendency is to take words and expressions at face value when, in fact, much more—often unspoken or unwritten—may be going on under the surface.

TRANSLATION PLEASE

Scolding, criticism, and controlling often mask love in disguise. Laying a love filter over our mother's communications can help us translate what she really is saying. Proverbs 14:29 reminds us that we are wise to be longsuffering and look below the surface, interpreting what is actually being conveyed.

When she criticizes, it may mean that she has high ideals for herself and that our behavior or performance falls short of what she expects for herself and consequently for others. She may want what is best for us but sees what we are presently doing as something that isn't all that beneficial for us. The same is true when it comes to her attempts to control and manipulate. She wants to protect us or help us reach her ideal. When we don't, she wants to aid us in reaching her level of acceptance.

All these actions communicate love, though it is masked and may be self-centered. The control and the criticism short-circuit the message.

Good communication means removing distractions and focusing fully on the other person and, very importantly, not formulating a rebuttal while that person is trying to talk to us. When relationships are not what they should be, we often go on the defensive. This immediately creates a barrier that prevents our ability to hear what the person is actually saying.

Developing skills as an active listener can help you communicate better. Your mother needs to know you care about her, so when she's trying to tell you something that really matters, give indicators that you are really listening. Even if you disagree or are not interested in the topic, you can have the courtesy to affirm the importance of her message by giving an occasional nod or an encouraging "uh-huh" to let her know you care.

Active listening also involves giving feedback and repeating back in your own words what you've understood the other person has said. Follow up by asking questions in order to clarify that you and your mom agree on what is being conveyed. If at all possible, allow her to finish without interruptions. In some cases—such as with nonstop talkers—this isn't possible. You may need to interject your responses between topics, stopping her and pulling her back to the first topic before she's on to the next.

By becoming an active listener, we convey respect and understanding. Respond truthfully and honestly to what is being said. This isn't always easy to do, because the tendency when we are frustrated is either to fall back into our role as the submissive child because we grew up under that, or to be overly assertive, treating our parent as the child. Though we may no longer be under the parent-child authority, we still need to respond with respect.

This isn't to say that we should bury our feelings or ignore issues. Doing so usually causes problems to grow until they become elephant-size.

PEACEMAKING OR CONFRONTATION?

It's taken years for you and your mom's relationship to get to where it is now. Over time, habits have been formed as you both learned to cope with one another's differences. For some daughters, the coping strategy is to confront and challenge when their opinion and mode of operating differ with their mother's. This rarely works, because it puts Mom on the defensive and creates a hostile, even explosive environment.

Others handle the differences by holding their tongues and doing whatever it takes to keep the peace. Still others choose to ignore the issues, pretending they don't exist. Letting matters go for too long creates elephant-size issues.

Allender and Longman in their book Bold Love note,

> Many people ignore the harm done to them and call it "forgiving" the other. In fact, one reason it may be ignored is the fear of causing conflict. When fear of the other is the undergirding motive for turning the other cheek, it cannot be called love, or forgiving the other. A lot of activity that is seen as spiritual is infused with fear, pretense, and ritual. The take-care-of-yourself movement accurately sees the potential for what appears to be loving behavior to be based on a heart that is not

concerned with love, but with protecting the self or others from difficult truths.[2]

Dennis Johnson observes,

Love discerns between petty issues that should be overlooked and substantive issues that must be resolved for genuine peace to reign. If you decide an issue needs addressing, repent from fear and move into dangerous territory if you want genuine resolution and not some facade. "God's peace does not peacefully coexist with falsehood, sham, or injustice; so God's peacemakers cannot simply ignore peace-destroying sin and error, any more than a surgeon can simply close up an infected wound: an abscess is bound to develop."[3]

James 1:26 reminds us to keep a tight reign on our tongues. "If anyone considers himself religious and yet does not keep a tight rein on his tongue, he deceives himself and his religion is worthless."

It's easy in the heat of frustration to erupt by saying things that hurt the other person. We do need to learn to manage our tongues so that we don't wound the other person. Once a wound is inflicted, the damage is done, and it's very difficult to go back and make reparation. There are also times, however, when it's appropriate to speak up when something our mom says or does is causing problems for us. The trick is to know when to hold the tongue and when to speak up.

Carrie has learned to balance peacemaking and confrontation by both curbing her tongue and confronting her mother when necessary.

Mom and I get along well, and I'm even bold enough now to confront her on errant behaviors, ways of thinking, and so on that are troublesome for me; and I can do it in love. She receives it well—now. Not to say she always thanks me for calling her attention to these things, nor do I thank her for things she confronts in me and my behavior. At least not at the time.

If errant behaviors are creating problems and are left unchecked, we stay locked in an insufferable and hopeless situation. How do we go about confronting in a godly manner?

Christina has a good relationship with her mom. One reason for this is their openness and honesty with each other. If one of them does or says something that hurts the other or creates friction, they make sure to address it right away. "If we see a potential problem coming up, like something the other is doing that's hurting our feelings, we talk about it and move on."

Many troubled mother-daughter relationships never get to this point. Can you imagine what Christina and her mom's relationship would be like if they didn't talk things through? Christina has also learned the importance of setting boundaries. Again, if we let a behavior or situation go unchecked, it can create serious issues for all involved, including those on the periphery. This is especially true with controlling mothers.

SPEAK UP!

Christina also has good insight on controlling moms:

If your mother is overly involved in your life, set boundaries, at the same time thanking her for caring. Remember—some mothers are very distant. If your mother is distant, reach out to her on an upside to any challenge. Don't focus on the negative; emphasize the positive.

Don't clam up. Speak up! Confront conflict or issues in an honest but gentle manner. Proverbs 16:23 gives us wisdom on how to confront: "A wise man's heart guides his mouth, and his lips promote instruction." There is a difference between instruction and criticism. Instructing is sharing an experience or information that equips the other person in order to help him or her reach a goal or produce desired results. This positive knowledge most often involves reflection and preparation rather than spontaneity.

Criticism is fault-finding and points out the areas where a person doesn't measure up. It often happens on the fly. If we let God guide our hearts, praying over the matter before we respond, we'll avoid responding with criticism rather than instruction. When we simply respond rather than reflect, we are more likely to put our mother on the defensive and cause deep hurts.

One final important thing to remember if it is necessary to confront her is avoiding "you" language. If you say to your mother, "You need to stay out of my business and stop meddling," you've already set the stage for friction, because you've put her on the defensive by pointing the finger.

Jeannie found it necessary to confront her mother regarding an issue that had become a problem. For years Jeannie's uncle, her grandmother's youngest son, had lived next door to her grandmother. The grandmother unintentionally favored that side of the family. Jeannie's dad, who had moved to a different state, died at a relatively young age. Her grandmother's only surviving son—Jeannie's uncle—and his family became even more important to her grandmother.

Jeannie's mother eventually moved back to the area where her late husband's family resided and was invited to family Thanksgiving celebrations at Jeannie's uncle's house. After the uncle's death, his children began their own Thanksgiving traditions, and Jeannie's mother was not included. Jeannie's mother took that as an intentional snub.

Since the uncle had assumed responsibility for Jeannie's grandmother, he left guardianship of the grandmother to one of his daughters.

Jeannie's mom still kept close ties to her mother-in-law, bringing her groceries and stopping by to check on her. However, she constantly vented her frustration by finding fault with her niece and her family who were not present when Jeannie and her siblings gathered at her mom's. Her mother referred to the niece and her children as "that family" and criticized them at every opportunity. Jeannie understood her mother's hurt, but she felt her attitude was poisonous and unhealthy. Having suffered through countless sessions of criticizing and complaining, Jeannie felt it needed to stop.

The next time her mother lapsed into belittling the other side of the family while gathering with her own family, Jeannie asked her mom if she could speak with her privately.

Jeannie prayed for guidance, and said, "Mom, I understand your frustration. I know your feelings have been hurt, but whenever you talk about that side of the family it feels very hateful—like a character assassination." She pointed out that a young nephew had heard her mother's most recent outburst. "As a Christian, I am not comfortable with that. I prefer you not do that in my presence."

Jeannie's mother looked shocked, which was what Jeannie expected. Then her mother tried to justify her actions, but Jeannie again restated that she wasn't comfortable with that kind of talk.

We can't expect to change a person and shouldn't fall into criticizing the person in order to make him or her fit our ideal of what we think he or she should be. It is, however, important to speak up if a behavior is causing serious damage or if correcting the person will improve how we connect and communicate. All relationships need healthy boundaries to prevent them from becoming destructive.

Is there a matter between you and your mother that is inhibiting your relationship? Take it to God before you talk with your mother. It isn't always possible to chat with God before you speak with her, because sometimes there isn't time. You may need to speak up in the heat of the moment. If you are caught unaware, guard your tongue closely. Once something comes from your lips, you will have a difficult time erasing any damage.

The biggest problem I see is that there is a lack of understanding between mother and daughter, and the daughter just accepts that every criticism is written in stone. Some women are ill-equipped to be a mother and do not know how to communicate with their daughters. The daughter is afraid to communicate with her mother. The mother's own fears come out as criticism and disapproval when it may be just her own fears being foisted on the daughter. The mother criticizes and doesn't offer the daughter her approval, because she fears the daughter will make the wrong choice. I think if you have a mother like this, as an adult it is okay to set boundaries with her. Your treatment of her may be the gift you have to give, but you don't have to take the garbage if that is what she's giving you (Crys).

GET CREATIVE

Even our best efforts may go awry. Sometimes the other person isn't open to listening to what we have to say, or he or she may need time to process it. It was interesting for me as the parent of three to see how Gaby, my second youngest daughter, reacted to parental discussions when we needed to correct her behavior. Gaby has always been a strong-willed child, and I learned early on that the harder I pushed to get her to behave in a desired manner, the more likely she was to resist.

Over time I learned that what worked best was to point out what needed changing, suggest how that might happen, and then back off. She still resisted at first, but when I eased off and let her process the options, after several days she often came around to my way of thinking. The same approach is viable when Mother is resistant to hearing what I have to say. I don't keep hammering away, expecting the behavior to immediately change. I give her time to think about it.

Audrey's relationship with her own rebellious daughter taught her much about how to interact with unconditional love. These principles apply to our relationships with our daughters and with our mothers.

"Both sides have to determine that they will demonstrate love for the other person, regardless—no shunning and controlling. Forgiveness has to be up-to-date. Wire your mouth shut if you have to in order to keep from advising the other person unless he or she asks for advice" (Audrey).

If your mother's behavior needs to change for the welfare of all, don't be afraid to address it more than once in a gentle manner. If it involves setting boundaries, don't back down. Stick to the parameters you have set, but remind your mother that those are your rules, and have a set consequence if she breaks them. For instance, in chapter 4 Linda talked about the boundaries she had set when her mother—who had control issues—came to visit. Linda had determined that her mother's attempt to criticize her and her husband's parenting was not acceptable. Whenever her mother started in, she received a warning that they wouldn't tolerate it, and she would have to go home if she kept at it. Her mother had to comply, or the visit was terminated.

Sometimes despite sincere attempts to talk through matters, you may find that your words have not been received. Your mother may simply not be able to understand or accept the problem. You may never be able to get through to her. It's easy to fall into despair when you want so desperately to build better connections, but if the other person isn't ready, willing, or even capable, it's not going to happen.

Put it on paper. I know several women who deal with difficulties in their relationships with their mothers by writing. I did this several years ago when I had reached the boiling point of frustration with my mom. I had tried to talk to her about some concerns that were bothering me, but my mother just didn't get it. So I sat down at the computer and vented in a letter. I wrote about the problems, the hurts, and how I longed to have her as a friend. Mailing such a letter would have been a mistake, because there were many deep hurts put down on that page, and the bitterness was evident. Instead, I tore it up and threw it away. There was something freeing about doing it, because it allowed me to express everything that was troubling me.

Work it out through writing. Journaling is another great way to express yourself. The content in a sense is like unmailed letters.

Whether letters or journals, putting observations and concerns on paper allows us to get in touch with our own feelings, frustrations, and longings and provides a way to vent them in a healthful manner.

Take it to God. One of the greatest outlets for working through broken relationships and communication is to convey it to the greatest listener of all. Isn't it good to know that when we talk to God, He is always available and ready to listen? Often, though, our conversations with God are like our one-way, broken-down conversations with people. For the communication to be conveyed well and clearly understood, we must not only talk but also listen. To hear what God is telling us, we have to shut out the noise that prevents us from listening. One of the biggest culprits is busyness.

Today's schedules are really hectic. We have cell phones, televisions, computers, and radios that interfere with hearing His voice, and we rush from one commitment to another. If we truly want to hear His guidance, we have to practice *being* more than *doing.* Being involves a state of peaceful existence, and to have this, we need a quiet place. A daily quiet time with God during which we can read His Word, reflect on it, talk to Him, and listen to Him will sharpen our listening skills. All of this is important, because it means we can take difficult matters—even seemingly hopeless relationships—to Him for advice, and He will guide our decisions and actions.

Katie realizes the importance of gaining an understanding of who our mothers are outside of their mothering roles. Too often we see our moms as just moms. Katie says,

> Stop looking at your mom as your mom. Start seeing her as a person—a woman who, even though you might not think it, has interests, hobbies, opinions, feelings, struggles, dreams, regrets, and beliefs all her own. Ask her about these. Remember: she existed before you. She had a life before you were born. Learn who she is apart from her being your mother. Search for the good, and forgive the bad. Pray for her.

COPING WITH CONFLICT

It's impossible to go through life without facing conflict. If we are honest with our emotions, we have to agree that it is also a part of relationships. From time to time we face circumstances that pit our wills against someone else's. This can especially be true in strained mother-daughter relationships. We may have learned to cope by avoiding conflict (flight) in order to keep the peace, or we may face the opposition with nails out and teeth barred (fight), determined to stand our ground.

Some people, including our mothers, have a knack for finding fault with even the tiniest thing, and when we are constantly subjected to criticism, it can rob us of our joy and create a breeding ground for turbulence, just as high and low pressure systems induce storm conditions.

The next time conflict rises between you and your mother, look at it as an opportunity to grow your character. If you can learn healthy ways to respond to conflict with her, it will work to everyone's benefit. The following are some things to remember.

First, practice humility. Don't become incensed when you feel you've been wronged. Don't retaliate. It will only stir up more ill feelings. Set aside a defensive mind-set; stop telling yourself you've been wronged and that you have a right to win. Be supportive. Respect your mother's opinion and ways of looking at matters, even if you think she is wrong and that you would handle them differently.

If we learn how to handle differences and improve communication with our Heavenly Father, listening as well as talking, we will also improve our communication skills and ability to relate to others, including our earthly parents.

This week as you go about your usual routine, consider the things you learned about your mother while working through this chapter. Hopefully they will deepen your compassion and understanding regarding why she does the things she does as well as assist you in knowing how to respond and communicate with her.

HEALING THOUGHTS

1. Did your mother affirm you as you were growing up? Give an example. _____

_____

_____

2. Do you think it's realistic to expect your mother to change? If not, why not? _____

_____

_____

3. Why is patience so important when it comes to coping with differences between you and your mother? _____

_____

_____

4. Do you have an issue or area in which you feel you need to confront your mother? If so, explain. _____

_____

_____

5. If you indicated yes to question four, write out or talk out a possible way you can talk to your mother about the problem. What would the ideal, loving confrontation look like?

_____

_____

SEVEN

NAMING THE HURTS

What do you think of when alone at night?
Do not the things your mothers spoke about,
Before they took the candle from the bedside,
Rush up into the mind and master it,
Till you believe in them against your will?
—William Butler Yeats[1]

In the movie *Groundhog Day*, egocentric weatherman Phil Conners, played by Bill Murray, is assigned the job of covering the annual Ground Hog Day festivities in Punxsutawney, Pennsylvania, for the fourth year in a row. Connors is incensed, because he aspires to be something more than a weather forecaster and believes the task is beneath him. After finishing the assignment, he heads back to Pittsburgh but has to turn back because of a blizzard he failed to predict. He checks back into the bed and breakfast inn where he had been staying. When he awakens the next day, he finds he's back on Groundhog Day again with the same annoying song playing on the clock radio, "I've Got You, Babe," by Sonny and Cher.

Nothing Conners does changes his circumstances. Each morning he rises to the same song, in the same town, with the same day ahead of him. When he realizes he's doomed to stay in small-town purgatory indefinitely, he turns to hedonistic pleasures. This, however, wears thin. Slowly his outlook and attitude change, and he turns his energy toward doing good. Conners undergoes transformation for the better.

The despair and hopelessness women sometimes experience in their fractured relationships with their mothers often spring from a feeling of having lost something valuable. We cannot go back and relive the past, and we can't seem to move ahead to improve the relationship either. Like Phil Conners, we remain trapped in our own endless version of Groundhog Day from which we cannot escape.

Whenever a relationship falls short of what we believe it could be, we lapse into wishful thinking. If only the other person would behave a certain way. If only certain things hadn't happened between us. If only she would change this thing or that thing about herself, then we would be able to happily coexist with her.

The older we grow, the stronger our longing for restoration tends to become. We see our own aging magnified in our mother's appearance and actions. A mother who might have been fiercely independent suddenly begins to suffer from a faulty memory or fragile health. We may find our parent-child roles reversing as we step into the role of caregiver.

More than ever, we long for peaceful relationships, but they may still be elusive. Old hurts remain with us—wounds that won't heal. Thoughts of having to move Mom into our home or move closer to where she lives to keep tabs on her causes a knot in our stomachs. How will we ever survive without losing our sanity? Adding new responsibilities to an already tense relationship is sure to bring even more friction. If only we could find a way to close the gap.

For an improved relationship to be possible, healing has to take place in the deep places inside us. Before we can move toward any type of "cure," we will need to reach within and examine painful memories we've pushed to far recesses. Like the woman who visits the dentist because a bad tooth is making her life miserable, we may dread delving deep. Yet doing so can bring relief and wholeness.

I WISH MY MOTHER

In some ways hurts are like dreams. Dreams weave together the pains, events, and anxieties we experience and bring them to our subconscious as we sleep. We may think we are coping well during our waking hours, but our quirky and sometimes downright bizarre dreams may say otherwise.

A few mornings ago my husband, Jeff, upon waking told me he had had a very strange dream. He dreamed someone had ordered him to take a death pill, which he did as ordered. He remembered thinking, I should be dead, but I'm not dying.

I am no interpreter of dreams, but knowing what is currently going on in our lives, I'm not surprised at such a heavy dream on my husband's part. We've left dependable church ministry positions in California to start a Christian coffee shop ministry in North Carolina. While working on launching the coffee shop in the midst of the current economic downturn in the United States, we've been seeking loans from lending institutions that are no longer lending to startups. We've also been piecing together income from various part-time jobs. No wonder Jeff is dreaming about death pills!

Just as we submerge worries and thoughts that surface in our dreams, we may also bury and stuff hurts and frustrations. When someone's words or actions cut us, we react in one of several ways. We may lash back with hurtful words of our own, cry, or downplay the hurt, putting on a mask of bravery. Many of us develop unhealthful coping habits, shoving the hurts deep down inside. We may trick ourselves into believing we have dealt with them, while they in fact may be bubbling under the surface.

I don't relish going to the dentist, but for some reason the most appropriate illustrations I can tie into this discussion are in the realm of dentistry. If you've ever had a dental X-ray, you may be familiar with the heavy, insulated bib the dental hygienist places over you to protect you. For the wearer, it presents an odd feeling of both comfort and protection. But if worn too long, the weight can become almost stifling. When we stuff our emotions and hurts, they can become like that heavy X-ray bib, robbing us of our joy.

Below is a list of wishes for you to complete. The purpose isn't to resurrect or exacerbate bad feelings to be used as ammunition. The exercise is intended to help you express what is lurking under the surface. You may already be aware of some of these feelings, while others may be well-disguised. Begin with the words *I wish my mother* . . . Try putting into words longings you have regarding your relationship with your mother. Your wishes can pertain to the past, present, or future.

Here are some examples to get you started:

I wish my mother—had traveled to see her grandchildren instead of always expecting us to come see her.

I wish my mother—cared about what I do for a living. She never asks me about my work. I'm not even sure she knows what I do vocationally.

I wish my mother—wasn't so unrefined. A lot of what she does is inappropriate in public.

I wish my mother—liked to read so we could share stories and authors and talk about them.

Save in a safe place the list you create. We will talk in the next chapter more about what you wrote. Your list reveals that some of our deepest wounds are caused by those we love most.

We've already looked at a variety of factors that prevent relationships from being healthy and cause long-lasting hurts. It's important to note that the cuts that go deepest are those that connect us with feelings of shame.

ESCAPING THE BLAME OF SHAME

In their book *The Truth Shall Set You Free: A Spiritual Program for People Recovering from Codependency and Life's Losses,* Jack McGinnis and Barbara Shlemon observe,

Many of us experience various problems in our relationships—cracks in the interpersonal bridges between ourselves and the significant others in our lives. If these breaks are not properly repaired, we cannot process our emotions, and we may experience a lingering sense of shame.[2]

Just as our mother may be unaware that she is interacting with us in an unhealthful manner in order to fill a void, we may respond while feeling an undercurrent pulling our spirit toward despair.

A while back a newspaper article showed a photograph of beautiful, expensive homes in a development that had been condemned. The homes had been built near a large lake, and suddenly the land on which they were built started caving in. Several homes were pulled into the vortex of a massive sinkhole.

Sinkholes appear in places where the solid earth beneath them has suffered some sort of devastating destruction. Though the land surface above ground may look stable and solid, underneath the ground are pockets lacking solidity. As the earth settles, there is nothing to keep these houses on equal footing, and some experience devastating destruction.

In another similar story, I read about a mining town that was experiencing similar devastation due to tunnels that ran for miles underground. Years of excavation and careless inattention regarding where buildings were being erected caused several structures in the downtown area to fall into an enormous crater.

Just as these structures could not stand against the devastation in the hidden places, neither can we survive destructive incidents at the hand of childhood primary caregivers without lingering effects. The inflicted hurts may be intentional or unintentional on the part of the caregiver. We may remember it or may have shoved it into a corner of our minds, never to recall it again. Despite our best efforts to downplay these wounds, suffering this humiliation can create serious baggage for us to carry.

Many of us carry around a burden of shame caused by a past incident. When we make an error, rather than thinking we've made a mistake, we may instead say to ourselves, *I am a mistake.* We may also sense we have in some way disappointed our mothers—or fathers. This feeling can linger like a heavy blanket of despair in a parent-child relationship. As we work to restore our "bridges," it helps to ask, *Who have I disappointed or embarrassed?*

While working my way toward overcoming some personal self-destructive behaviors, I was encouraged to write down negative memories of incidents from my childhood that caused me to experience humiliation or shame. The feelings I recorded included humiliation, inadequacy, embarrassment, futility, imperfection, and inferiority. The picture isn't exactly one of a healthy self-image. I had no idea until I began my inward probing that I was carrying around such heavy baggage.

The outcome of the exercise surprised me. I had often blamed my mother for my feelings of inadequacy. After all, she rarely gave me any compliments or told me she loved me, and she was highly critical. But I could recall no particular singular incident that left a deep wound. Looking back, I see now that it was more a case of being subjected to daily barrages of criticism, not just of me but of everything my mother saw wrong with the world. It was like being subjected to the constant, annoying drip of a faucet.

I also realize that in some cases my siblings were the instigators of shaming incidents, and on other occasions my father was. This was a real shocker. By examining these hurtful recollections, I was able to bring them into the open and get some closure.

Shame has two faces. We may feel shame because of our own perceived shortcomings, or we may feel shame related to someone else's behavior. Rather than accusing ourselves of being a mistake, we may see the other person as an embarrassment or a mistake. Jennifer recounts feeling guilty because of these feelings toward her mother:

> There is a saying "You can take the girl out of the country, but you can't take the country out of the girl." This is very applicable to my mom. She still uses poor grammar, is not well-read, and is as simplistic, unscholarly, uncultured, and unpolished as she was when I was in high school. One never knows if at family

dinners she'll unabashedly belch or worse. She talks incessantly about nothing of great importance—even with complete strangers in the grocery store line.

I admit to struggling with feelings of embarrassment when it comes to my mom, and I'm not particularly proud of it.

Maybe you can identify with this type of shame. It's shaming to even admit to having such feelings. Here are a few questions to consider. Feel free to write down your answers:

1. How do you see your mother? Are you proud to be related to her, or are you embarrassed by her? _____

_____

_____

_____

2. If you often feel embarrassed by her, what does this say about your own shortcomings? _____

_____

_____

_____

3. If you could name the emotion at the core of this shame, what would it be? _____

_____

_____

In my case, I realize that pride is the foundation of my embarrassment. I am afraid of what people will think. If you get down to the crux of the matter, my response to my mother basically says that I think I am superior to my mom. That's not exactly a godly attitude, is it? James 4:6 says, "He gives us more grace. That is why Scripture says: 'God opposes the proud but gives grace to the humble.'"

Use the following exercise to name shaming incidents in your own life.

SHAMING EXPERIENCES

1. Use the space below to write out some shaming incidents that you recall from your childhood. _____

_____

_____

2. What feelings surfaced while you were remembering these experiences?

_____

_____

_____

3. Sometimes while trying to curb our behavior, our childhood caregivers said hurtful things. Do any of the following statements sound familiar? Circle the letter of the ones you remember. Use the extra space to write your own.

a. "You can do better than that."

b. "You're never going to amount to anything."

c. "You never learn, do you?"

d. "I've had it up to here with you!"

e. "I hope someday you'll have a kid just like you."

f. "Stop crying, or I'll give you something to cry *about*."

g. "Why don't you grow up?"

h. "Leave me alone. I've had a rough day."

i. "You're not trying."

j. "Why can't you be more like _____?"

k. "Shut up!"

l. "You make me sick."

m. "You call this clean?"

n. "Close the door. Were you raised in a barn?"

o. "You'll never amount to anything."

p. "I am so disappointed in you."

q. "This is the school we've chosen for you, and that's final."

Use the following space to write other hurtful sayings your parents used that might not be listed above. _____

_____

_____

_____

Now, beside the ones you circled and/or wrote in, write down a more positive way to say it. _____

_____

_____

_____

HEALING THOUGHTS

1. In what ways do we trick ourselves into believing we have dealt with hurts or shaming incidents? _____

_____

_____

_____

2. Would you say your mother has control issues? If so, what are some of them? Write down one or two examples. _____

_____

_____

_____

3. Have you ever been guilty of trying to control a child or someone else you love? If so, give an example below. _____

_____

_____

_____

4. How does it make you feel to talk about hurts you've experienced in your relationship with your mother? _____

_____

_____

_____

5. Name one thing you can do to move past some of these old wounds. _____

_____

_____

EIGHT

FORGIVING THE UNFORGIVABLE

Forgiveness does not change the past,
but it does enlarge the future.
—Paul Boese[1]

In order to manage their large family, Mike and Kathie Clarey had a strict schedule that kept things running like clockwork. Part of the routine included making sure their two middle daughters, Susie and Katie, were out of bed and traveling their separate morning newspaper routes before school. One morning Kathie roused the girls as usual, sending them on their way after breakfast. The first hint of something amiss came when a customer called complaining that he hadn't gotten his morning paper. He was on Katie's route. Kathie looked at the clock, and her chest tightened. Something was very wrong! Eleven-year-old Katie should have already been home.[2]

With a knot in his stomach and a growing sense of foreboding, Mike drove Katie's paper route looking for his little girl, but Katie had vanished. Fear rose in Mike's throat, and his knuckles whitened as he gripped the steering wheel. Turning the car to travel the familiar route again, he scanned the road and sidewalks for Katie. As he did so, a small bundle near the drive of a local carwash caught his eye—Katie's newspaper carrier bag.

Heart hammering, he threw the car in park and ran over to the object. His hands trembled as he lifted the bag. A groan of anguish escaped him. The bag was covered in blood. Mike rushed to a phone and called 911. What he learned a short while later shattered his family's lives. Detectives worked with eyewitnesses piecing together an account of what had transpired. The unthinkable had happened. Little Katie had been abducted, brutally assaulted, and murdered by a man with a history of sexual crimes.

In the wake of the tragedy, and with their lives in upheaval, the couple and their family found their devout faith challenged. They asked gut-wrenching questions of their Heavenly Father: "How could a loving God allow this to happen?" Still, in the midst of the storm, their faith held firm.

At one point during a frenzy of press interviews, one reporter pushed a microphone toward Kathie and posed a shocking question. "Do you have anything you would like to say to the man who killed Katie?"

She stood in stunned silence, tears glistening in her yes. Kathie swallowed hard. "Yes, we do. We would like to tell him we forgive him."

The darkness of a human soul who can do something as deplorable as raping and murdering a young child is inconceivable to us. Even more difficult to fathom is how someone could ever forgive such a heinous act. That truly is a strong faith.

We may never have something of this magnitude to forgive, but many of us have been gravely wounded. Some of these wounds have been inflicted by those who claim to love us, including our mothers.

Holding onto our deep hurts can freeze our ability to function in a healthy manner. It can also retard our spiritual growth and even cause us to move backward rather than growing toward maturity. We should by all purposes become better individuals as we allow God to work in our lives. If, however, there are areas of our lives we refuse to let go, particularly those that need healing, we may instead become bitter rather than better.

One of the things we will be looking at in this chapter is how to release our hurts and grudges. Jesus provided some insight regarding how to do that.

GENEROUS FORGIVENESS

One day as Jesus was teaching, Peter lobbed one of his usual straightforward questions at Him: "Lord, how many times shall I forgive my brother when he sins against me? (Matthew 18:21). Thinking he was the clever pupil, Peter even suggested what seemed like a generous number. "Up to seven times?"

Jesus' response surely took him by surprise: "seventy times seven" (verse 22, KJV). Surely that seems like a liberal amount, a whopping four hundred ninety times. Jesus often used exaggeration to make a point. Seventy times seven was an embellishment intended to let His listeners know that we are to generously forgive wrongdoings. He certainly didn't mean that we are to literally stop forgiving a person after he or she has topped four hundred ninety transgressions.

Can you imagine what it would be like if God's forgiveness mirrored the way credit card companies with their credit limits operate? "Sorry—your credit line is frozen," He might say. "You've maxed out your forgiveness credit."

Fortunately, God doesn't operate that way. There's no limit to His forgiveness of our wrongdoing. We are urged to "Be imitators of God, therefore, as dearly loved children and live a life of love, just as Christ loved us and gave himself up for us as a fragrant offering and sacrifice to God" (Ephesians 5:1). We are to imitate Him. When we model our lives after the Father and His Son, we also emulate their inexhaustible capacity to forgive.

The Clareys mirrored Jesus' sacrificial forgiveness when they forgave Katie's murderer. Jesus in His last excruciating moments of suffering on the Cross forgave those responsible for putting Him there, even when He had done nothing wrong. His words "Father, forgive them, for they do not know what they are doing" (Luke 23:34) still pierce our hearts today.

The hurts we have suffered from our mother's words, actions, or callousness may seem vast. Because hurtful patterns create ruts that run deeply, the hurts keep happening. It may seem to us that our mother has exceeded her quota for being forgiven. Each time it happens again, the wounds reopen, and we feel them afresh. How can we forgive when the hurts continue on?

God waits ever so patiently for us, reminding us that He is here for us. "Come to me, all you who are weary and burdened, and I will give you rest" (Matthew 11:28). We are to bring these hurts to Him and place them on His back.

I work in a local women's ministry that provides a day shelter and residential program for women who might otherwise go homeless. They have many deep emotional wounds and needs. Some come out of abuse or chemical dependency. Some are ex-offenders. Destructive patterns and brokenness are deeply ingrained, and as much as we would like to keep and nurture them all in order to protect them, sometimes they make such poor decisions while in our program that we have to ask them to leave.

This is heart-wrenching for all our staff. After one particularly rough week in which chaos and complications abounded, we had to make a tough call regarding one woman we all cared about deeply. One of my coworkers was particularly heartbroken. She had a special place in her heart that resonated with this lost child. Everything within her cried out to let this woman stay, because she feared what might happen to her after she exited the program. Yet she knew that in order to help her and not enable her destructive behavior, she had to agree with the rest of the professional staff's decision. They asked this resident to leave the program.

Knowing what had just transpired, I walked into this coworker's office and found her crying. Her tear-stained face and sagging shoulders reflected her fatigue and anguish. I offered what felt like feeble words of comfort, dabbing her mascara-blurred eyes with a tissue and holding her as she cried. As I stood with my arms embracing her with compassion, I realized that this is what the Father does for us. He is willing to share our pain with us so we don't have to bear it by ourselves. What a comfort to know He is there to wrap His arms around us and dry our tears!

RELEASING THE BURDEN

How do we find rest from our brokenness and burdens? How do we come to a place where we can forgive? In the last chapter we focused on writing a wish list of how we would like for our relationships with our mothers to be. We also reflected on matters that caused us to feel shame and hurt.

Naming the hurts is the first step in moving toward healing, but sometimes the hurts run so deeply that they have produced grudges. Once resentment takes hold, it can poison our attitude and even morph into hatred. We've all seen people so bent on righting a wrong that their lives are consumed with it.

I read about an American Jew who had survived the Nazi Holocaust. He had devoted his life to tracking down those who had been involved in these horrendous war crimes. I know I will never understand suffering and hurt of the magnitude that the Jews in the concentration camps suffered, but I question the focus this person had on seeking revenge. That someone would devote his life to vengeance seems a waste of God's purpose for him.

In their book *The Truth Shall Set You Free*, mentioned earlier, Jack McGinnis and Barbara Shlemon discuss the importance of sincerely forgiving our offenders. We're all familiar with the saying "Forgive and forget."

For forgiveness to truly happen, we have to acknowledge what *really* happened, because our memories are often faulty. When the painful incident occurred, we may have acted as if it didn't happen or may have even stuffed our emotions. It's also possible that we blamed the wrong person for causing the pain.

"We may make an effort to forgive our parents or other primary caregivers for hurting us before we have acknowledged and dealt with our anger, hurt, and fear," McGinnis and Shlemon write.

When we experience hurts, we also experience loss. Someone's words or actions can cause us to grieve or be angry. Wounds can kill our joy, create brokenness, and prevent us from living a balanced and fulfilled life. It's important for us to have a clear picture of what happened in order to move past it. Otherwise, we may experience anger, fear, or hurt without clearly understanding why those emotions are present in us.

Take a moment to look over the notes you made in chapter 7. In your wish list you put down things that you felt were missing in your relationship with your mother. For instance, in my case I wrote, "I wish my mother were a better listener." If we honestly look at what we have written, we can interpret our feelings as a wrong or an offense committed against us by our mother. In some cases it's the sins of omission, what she failed to do, as much as the sins of commission, things she actually did, that were wrong or hurtful.

Following are some steps you can take to work your way toward forgiving her. With enough practice, this can help you cope with any future wrongs you feel your mother has done to you.

1. Look over your wish list and your journal of shaming incidents. Be as detailed as possible when recalling what happened.

2. Consider a specific incident and how it unfolded. Do this with as many offenses as possible. Make notes if necessary. Take a moment now to work on that.

3. Once you have done that, look again at what you have written. For each incident, consider why your mother may have acted the way she did.

4. In each of these cases, write how you felt when it happened (if you haven't already). Use this same process each time something similar happens.

5. Don't take what your mother did or failed to do personally. Chances are, if she interacted with you this way, she's also interacted

with others in a similar fashion, so you're not the only one to be hurt.

6. Remember that every person is human, including you, so you are bound to fall short.

7. Pray and ask God to forgive her. You do not need to divulge this to your mother.

A HEART LIKE THE FATHER'S

The parable of the prodigal (Luke 15:11-31) is one with which most of us are familiar. It shows a father's forgiveness for the unthinkable hurts his son inflicted. We're introduced to this selfish younger son, who has a sense of entitlement. He knows he will receive his part of his inheritance after his father passes away, but being young and full of wild aspirations, he can't wait to get his hands on the money so he can live the lifestyle he aspires to.

He insults his father by demanding his inheritance while his father is still alive. Like many a parent with headstrong children, the father knows there's heartache on the horizon if he hands over the money. But he also knows there's no arguing with this strong-willed child, so he complies.

Sure enough, what the father imagines happening does. The son goes off to a foreign land, spends all the money on partying and possessions, and blows through it faster than a car full of joy-riding teenagers at a traffic light.

Then, when he hits rock bottom and finds himself hungry and destitute, taking the only job he can find—feeding pigs—he comes to his senses and returns to his father to ask for forgiveness.

This amazing, loving father not only welcomes his son home, but he also throws a party for him. The parable is meant to show us how valuable we are to the Father. Though we may be strong-willed and sinful, He is waiting for us to turn and repent. When we do, He welcomes us with loving arms.

The story also shows us the heart of the Father. He is willing to forgive the unforgivable. If God can be this forgiving to us who have hurt Him so deeply, surely we also must forgive the deep hurts we've experienced. Doing so allows us to let go of the hurts we have suffered and move toward wholeness.

I was not able to begin to repair the relationship with my mother until I forgave her for what I perceived that she did wrong. For me, the hardest part was admitting to myself that I was angry. Once I took that step, I was able to begin a process of forgiveness, and that changed the way I viewed my mother. That led to healing and reconciliation in our relationship. I have not arrived yet, but I'm finding it easier and easier to forgive her when I feel slighted by her (Sarah).

Eileen, who in chapter 7 shared her attempt to restore her relationship with her mom, eventually made some progress:

I finally went home and saw my mom after over two years. I told her I was sorry we didn't have a good relationship and felt bad that it seemed as though we wouldn't. I told her I forgave her and asked once again that she forgive me. Then I left. I let my mom process that for a while and slowly started to reestablish contact with her. God led me to the right man, whom I married and who has been instrumental in helping me restore and rebuild this relationship. He actually prayed with my mom a few years back to get saved. I now talk to her several times a week. It isn't a deep relationship, but it's much better than it ever was. It's up to me to walk in love toward my mom and show her the love of God.

If we had total control of our lives, we would choose not to have hurts inflicted on us. Even when we work to repair the damage, it is still nearly impossible to erase memories associated with those hurts. What we can do is address those hurts and move past the memories. It is much better to be forward-looking than backward-gazing, operating like concentration camp survivors, dwelling on the past.

We're reminded in 1 Peter 4:8, "Above all, love each other deeply, because love covers over a multitude of sins." The love of the Father is in us. The deeper the wound, the longer it takes to heal. We must be patient, allowing God to work through us as we work toward wholeness in ourselves and our relationships.

HEALING THOUGHTS

1. What does Kathie Clarey's ability to forgive her daughter's murderer tell you about Kathie? _____

_____

_____

_____

2. How do you feel when you are with someone who has a bitter attitude? _____

_____

_____

_____

3. How can you forgive someone who has hurt you when he or she keeps inflicting new wounds? _____

_____

_____

_____

4. How did you feel after working through the shaming incident exercise above? _____

_____

_____

_____

5. What additional actions can you take in order to forgive your mother? _____

_____

_____

_____

NINE

BECOMING THE CHANGE WE WANT TO SEE

———————————◆———————————

What the daughter does, the mother did.
—Jewish proverb[1]

While a man's hearing was being tested, the electricity went off. Facing a lengthy delay because of a blown transformer, the technician performing the exam had little choice but to reschedule the man's test. She assured him that he would not be charged for the second exam, but a week later after having completed the rescheduled hearing test, the gentleman received an invoice in the mail for the second appointment. Stomach knotting in frustration, he called the insurance company but immediately landed in "phone purgatory." He pushed phone buttons for menu choices until he reached a live agent.

"Thank you for calling customer service. This is Cindy. How can I help you?" The rep's monotone greeting conveyed apathy, the apparent product of helping countless dissatisfied customers day after day. She asked for preliminary information, and her tone changed from disinterest to impatience to brusqueness when her client couldn't immediately locate his insurance number. "Hold a moment while I check on some information," she said, cutting him off in mid-sentence before he could fully explain.

He waited several minutes, drumming his fingers impatiently on the desk while Christmas elevator music played annoyingly in the background. Several minutes later the agent came back on the line. "Hi—sorry to keep you holding. I'm going to have to do more research. We'll be closed for the Christmas holidays. The earliest we can get back to you is the first week of January."

He clinched his fist in frustration and swallowed the remark tingling on the end of his tongue. Losing his cool would only exacerbate the situation. In as kind a voice as he could muster, he responded, "That will be fine. Call me when it's convenient. Have a Merry Christmas."

The agent's voice warmed to his courteous response, and she wished him the same before hanging up. Less than two hours later, and to the man's delight, the agent called back, informing him that she had taken care of the matter. He told her how thrilled he was with the fast response.[2]

The agent's surly attitude could have quickly changed the policyholder into an irate customer. But instead of giving into anger, he chose to answer with kindness. His gentle response motivated the insurance agent to change her own outlook.

We are frequently told it's nearly impossible to change anyone but ourselves, and this often proves to be true. If you picked up this book hoping to change your mom, you may be sorely disappointed. It is nigh impossible to control how someone else acts. Your mom has had years to develop patterns of behavior and may be either happy the way things are or oblivious to any improvements she may need to make.

Since changing your mother may be too much to ask, your focus should be on modifying how you think about her and respond to her. Altering how you interact with others may not seem to affect them directly, but it can impact them enough to create "ripples" that move out from you, the instigator of that change, and touch them as well. Before anything of the kind can take place, the metamorphosis has to happen in you, and it begins with a change of attitude.

Earlier I pointed out that we can become either bitter or better. How we respond to our circumstances greatly affects our outlook. If we blame others for every hurt or wrong in our lives, we condemn ourselves to a miserable existence. Abraham Lincoln wisely observed, "Most folks are about as happy as they make up their minds to be."[3]

Despite your efforts, your mother may keep handling matters in the same old way. Since change is unlikely, it's up to you to become the change you want to see. Transformation won't happen overnight but rather in small baby steps.

In the movie *What About Bob?* Bob Wiley, played by Bill Murray, is a neurotic man with many hang-ups and phobias.[4] He's so fearful that he must talk himself into stepping outside his apartment any time he needs to venture out. Bob also can't make a move without the advice of his psychiatrist and has become so troublesome to his present doctor that the psychiatrist refers him to a successful colleague, Leo Marvin (Richard Dreyfuss) in order to be rid of him.

Dr. Marvin agrees to take Bob on and coaches him, explaining that the change Bob desires is up to him. It's a matter of making baby steps. Shortly after Bob begins going to Dr. Marvin, the doctor informs him that he's leaving for vacation. He provides Bob with emergency contact info should he need help while he's out of town. At the end of the session the doctor shoves his recently published book into Bob's hands, advises him to read it, and wishes him well.

As you might have guessed, Bob doesn't cope well in the doctor's absence and in desperation uses trickery to determine the doctor's vacation whereabouts. One of the most comical scenes is when Bob steps off the bus in the small resort town with Gil, his pet goldfish, hanging from his neck in a goldfish bowl. Not long after, Bob tracks down Dr. Marvin, whose life he proceeds to make miserable.

The hilarious movie shows how out-of-control neediness can be, but it also reveals an important truth. Most change is up to us, and it rarely happens all at once. Change must happen a little at a time in baby steps.

IT STARTS WITH FORGIVENESS

The difficult things we have been through, the hurts and wrongdoings we have experienced, are valid and real. Nevertheless, in order for us to change, we must be willing to deemphasize them, taking on a positive attitude so we can move forward. Focusing on the negative and clinging to the hurts will keep us in the same rut. This is especially true when it comes to interacting with our mothers. Matthew 18:21-23 shows us how to put forgiveness into practice.

Remember the question Peter asked Jesus about how many times we should forgive, and Jesus' reply—"seventy times seven"? Jesus backed up His answer with an illustration. See Matthew 18:21-35, and take a moment to read the story now.

The king represents God. The indebted servant represents us. One day as the king was working on his accounts, he decided to make it a day of reckoning for all his subjects who were indebted to him. He probably started with the most significant debt, summoning one particular servant who owed him ten thousand talents. This was no small sum. In Jesus' day a talent was worth approximately $15,000, the equivalent of millions of dollars by today's standard.[5]

As you might imagine, if any of us owed such a large sum, it would be almost impossible for us to pay off such a debt. In those days when a man fell behind in paying his debts, the noble or king to whom he owed the money had the right to seize the man's property, including his family, and dispose of them as he pleased in order to regain some of what was owed to him.

The debt in the story is symbolic of our shortcomings. We are all born as sinners, and like the servant in the story, we fall short. There is no way we can pay the king—our Heavenly Father—the debt we owe Him for sending Jesus, His only Son to die for us. By all rights, we should be in the same hopeless position as the indebted servant, but we are saved by God's incredible grace.

When the servant learned of the king's intent to seize his family and possessions, he fell at the king's feet and begged for mercy. He must have been very convincing, for the king was filled with compassion. He did the unthinkable and forgave the servant his debt. Can you imagine your reaction if someone of power came to your rescue and paid off your car, your mortgage, and all your other debts? The servant was surely stunned.

One would think that after being shown such mercy, the forgiven servant would have been a changed man, showing the same kindness and mercy to others. But once his debts were paid, the servant saw it as an opportunity to improve his own financial standing. He located a servant who owed him a hundred denarii, the equivalent of just a few dollars. The servant who had begged for mercy just a short while earlier stood over the miserable servant and demanded his money.

Just as the forgiven servant had pleaded with the king for mercy, this servant pleaded for mercy from the man who had been forgiven. But his plea fell on deaf ears. Instead, the forgiven servant threw the man into prison. When the king learned of what had happened, he was furious. He condemned the unforgiving servant to prison and ordered that he be tortured until he could pay his debt.

Jesus concluded this story with a sobering warning (verse 35): "This is how my heavenly Father will treat each of you unless you forgive your brother from your heart."

What does this mean for us—that we should beware of holding someone's wrongdoings against him or her? Yes, but it also means we can never repay the debt of forgiveness we owe God—and that knowledge should create in us a forgiving spirit toward others. Our human nature makes us want to nurse our hurts and hold them against those who inflicted them on us. How can we release the grievances we have against others?

Forgiveness must enter the picture in our relationships. We have to forgive our moms and other loved ones not only for what they've done but also for what they haven't done—but we also need to forgive ourselves. Maybe, too, we should learn to relax on the subject of understanding and being understood and simply learn to accept and appreciate each other as we are. Stress the positives and try to sweep the negatives under the rug after we're done mulling them over and hashing and rehashing them. Maybe they can be put to rest and we can go about living the rest of our lives for the Lord (Yvonne Joan Hill).

WE CAN SHOW WE CARE THROUGH PRAYER

But I tell you: Love your enemies and pray for those who persecute you, that you may be sons of your Father in heaven. He causes his sun to rise on the evil and the good, and sends rain on the righteous and the unrighteous. If you love those who love you, what reward will you get? Are not even the tax collectors doing that? (Matthew 5:44-46).

It's easy to love those who love us, but it's much harder to love those who are difficult to love. Prayer helps soften the heart and produce a metamorphosis. When we take our concerns to God, we can ask not only for our own transformation but for the transformation of others as well. As we lay these concerns before the Lord, He begins to chip away at the scar tissue on our heart that prevents us from caring more deeply for that other person.

Marie recognized that prayer was a key to transformation in her own relationship with her mother. "I've finally accepted that I can't do anything about what she thinks and does, but I can control my own thoughts and actions. Through prayer and working hard at my own walk with the Lord, I can handle whatever comes my way."

How can we pray?

Start by thanking Him. The story is told of parents who had two children. One child was always depressed, looking at the world through dark-colored glasses. Her sister was just the opposite and created her own rainbow-colored reality. No one should be that happy, thought the parents. Surely this child is out of touch with her emotions.

Christmas was fast approaching. The parents decided a change of attitude was in order for both of their daughters. They gave the pessimistic daughter everything she wanted for Christmas plus much more. As she opened present after present, the little girl found something to complain about regarding every gift.

To the other optimistic daughter they gave only one gift, a wrapped box of manure. The daughter tore into the box and began digging down with her hands, scooping out handfuls of the foul-smelling stuff, laughing and smiling all the while. "Thank you, Mom and Dad. This is just what I wanted." Her parents looked at each other with puzzled expressions.

"Honey," said the mother, "that's just a box of manure."

"I know," replied the daughter, lifting out another handful, "but there's a pony in here somewhere."

If only we could take on the attitude of the optimistic child, digging through the manure in order to find the pony.

What are some of the positive things you can thank God for regarding your mother? Does she stay in touch? Did she make your clothes when you were a child? Does she love to cook for you? How does she show her love? Focus only on the good things, and thank God for them.

Pray for your attitude. Ask God to help you change your attitude toward her and point out when you are not being positive. "We demolish arguments and every pretension that sets itself up against the knowledge of God, and we take captive every thought to make it obedient to Christ" (2 Corinthians 10:5).

Ask God to change her. Though you cannot change your mother, God can. Keep praying for her, imploring God to work on her heart and attitude. Pray specifically regarding things that you feel need changing.

Ask God to help you forgive. If you are having difficulty moving past some of your hurts, ask God to help you let go of them. The more you take these needs to Him, the easier it will be to let go.

MINIATURES OF CHRIST

To truly be transformed, we must model Christlike character. Contrary to what many believe, being like Christ doesn't mean we have to be meek wimps. We've probably all seen artwork depicting Jesus as passive and even a little effeminate—not a very realistic depiction of God's Son. Christ was bold and compassionate, filled with truth and grace. He confronted people with the truth, challenging them to alter not only their behavior but also their attitudes, even when He knew it would make Him appear unfavorable in their eyes. Despite this hard side, He was also tenderhearted and forgiving. He confronted only when the situation necessitated it.

This, then, is our model for attitude and behavior. Replicating Christ means working at understanding, accepting, and loving people. It doesn't necessarily mean we condone what they do or say. We recognize them for who they are but believe in what they could be. It's difficult to model Christ when we are under fire from the person we love. For some of us, appreciating our mother will be like looking for the pony in that box of manure. Learning to love someone who is difficult to love is like looking at someone through a telescope. It makes even the smallest positives seem substantial. This is how God sees us and how He wants us to look at others.

A young college graduate was experiencing much anger toward her mother, who lived several states away. When she talked to a friend about her feelings, she blamed her parents for being unfair with how they mediated disagreements between her older sister and her when she was growing up.

"They always took my sister's side." She also divulged that she held it against them for not standing up for her when she was bullied by some girls in school. "They made my life miserable, and my parents didn't do anything. I don't care if I stay in touch with my parents, because frankly I don't even know if I love them. I don't feel anything for them."

"Did you ever tell your mom you were being bullied?" asked her friend. "Did the school tell your parents?"

"I didn't tell my mom because I didn't feel safe confiding in her. They were always judging me and spouting scripture. I don't know if the school ever let her know about the bullying."

This young woman's mother was hurt by her daughter's decision to withhold contact because she "felt no love for her." Had she chosen to call her mom and talk about her hurts, she might have been able to rebuild the relationship. Instead, she chose to cling to the past. Some might say that acting as if you love someone is phony. But practicing love can actually soften our hearts toward that person. By acting out love, we sew seeds that can grow into the genuine thing.

Being Christlike means practicing kindness and humility even when we are not on the receiving end of it. It also means getting control of anger. In 1 Corinthians 13:5, 7 Paul writes about love: "It is not rude, it is not self-seeking, it is not easily angered, it keeps no record of wrongs. . . . It always protects, always trusts, always hopes, always perseveres."

Christlike love also means taking a bold stand when necessary, especially on the other person's behalf. Most important, Christlike love reveals a long-suffering nature, a nature willing to forgive countless times. If you want to see what true love looks like, read the complete chapter of 1 Corinthians 13.

Leslie noted, "Things between us changed the most when God helped me to see my mother as a woman—a person who got where she is through her own life history—with scars, fears, and needs. It still grates on me when she starts in about some problem member of the family, but now I see her differently, and we've shared some very special moments."

Accepting someone else's idiosyncrasies and shortcomings is grace in action.

GETTING HELP WHEN WE ARE STUCK

Sometimes despite our desire for healing, deep hurts bind us where we are. I know several women who have struggled with pain from the past, pain in which their mothers had a hand. One woman was sexually abused by a relative and blamed her mother for not being aware of it. Another came out of a family relationship with an alcoholic father where there was a lot of verbal abuse and dysfunction. Her daughter wrestled with feelings of hurt because her mother allowed not only her but also her children to be subjected to the hurt.

If you feel you still have issues you are unable to move past, you may need professional counseling in order to move on. Jeff and I have been to Christian counselors on several occasions, a few times for marital struggles and on other occasions to work through personal issues. Those sessions were pivotal points for us that helped us gain a perspective on challenges and assisted us in developing a plan for how to cope and change.

Many people avoid counseling because they feel they either can't afford it or are afraid of what other people will think, or they believe it signifies they aren't as spiritual as they should be. When we were trying to sell our house in California, we had to make numerous changes in order to prepare it for the market. Our real estate agent reminded us that the money we were paying into the house was not an expense but an investment. Making those changes would make the house more sellable and desirable.

Counseling, in much the same way, is not an expense but an investment. It takes the "house" we live in and renovates it so it is wholesome and healthy. If cost is holding you back, be advised that many churches have free lay counseling programs that can help you work through concerns. In addition, some professional counselors have sliding-scale fees or discounts they offer.

There is nothing shameful about going to a counselor for help. In fact, admitting your weaknesses is actually a sign of strength. A counselor is a trained listener and observer who can provide objective feedback and direction to help you work through issues preventing you from moving on. Don't be afraid to seek help. Doing so can help you get "unstuck" and speed restoration to relationships.

If we remain in Christ and He remains in us, we cannot help but take on a more Christlike nature, because we remain connected to Him. By continuing our relationship with Christ, we ensure an improved relationship with everyone with whom we come in contact. "Remain in me, and I will remain in you. No branch can bear fruit by itself; it must remain in the vine. Neither can you bear fruit unless you remain in me" (John 15:4).

Sometimes our awareness of what we need to change doesn't come until we mature more in our relationship with Christ. One woman who had always wrestled with her relationship with her mom suddenly saw her own shortcomings as she exhibited similar behaviors with her own daughter.

After my mother's death, I began to realize things I didn't see before. I saw where I had hurt her when I withdrew from her. When my adult daughter hurt my feelings, I thought I remember saying those very things to my mother (Margaret).

We can delve into our mother's past, learn more about her personality, work on communication, confront her, and even set boundaries when necessary. Despite all these efforts, some mothers will not change because they are not capable of doing so.

If this is the case, we will have to grow our tolerance and become more willing to accept her as she is in order to make the relationship work. It's biblical and Christlike, but not necessarily easy. Just remember: through Christ all things are possible.

In his book *Changes that Heal*, Henry Cloud writes,

It is literally never too late to open up to those who love us and care about our development. Because the aspect of ourselves that goes outside of time in childhood gets stored in its chronological state, it is still that same age when it returns. God can use our current relationships to provide the nurturing we didn't receive as children, the mentoring we missed as school-age kids, or the companionship we needed as teenagers. God can and does redeem the time for us; there is nothing sacred about "the first time around." Because time is experience, we can influence any "past" aspect of ourselves in the present. In the present we can reach the hurting, lonely child of our past. The lonely child, the hurting child, the untrained child, and whoever else we "were" is still alive; he or she is eternal and lives within us.[6]

HEALING THOUGHTS

1. If you want someone to change, what action should you take?

_____

_____

_____

2. According to Matthew 18:21-22, what does the Bible say about people who don't forgive those who have wronged them?

_____

_____

_____

3. Why is forgiveness a large part of being able to change?

_____

_____

_____

4. Have you ever been guilty of withholding love from someone because you were hurt or angered by him or her? What were the circumstances? _____

_____

_____

_____

5. Why is it important to get outside help if we cannot move past our hurts? _____

_____

_____

TEN

BECOMING A CHANGE AGENT

Treat people as if they were what they ought to be, and you help them to become what they are capable of being.
—Goethe[1]

Back in the early 1950s scientists studying Macaca Fuscata monkeys on the island of Koshima, Japan, fed the monkeys raw sweet potatoes by dropping the treats in the sand. The monkeys loved the sweet potatoes but did not like having to swallow the grit that stuck to the potatoes.[2] One smart little monkey decided the solution was to wash off her sweet potatoes in a nearby stream.

She taught this trick to her mother and peers, who began washing their sweet potatoes before eating them too. Soon other young monkeys learned the trick and taught their parents the skill as well. By the time the behavioral change reached the hundredth monkey, all the monkeys in that particular tribe were washing their sweet potatoes. The monkeys then passed on this habit to other colonies of monkeys who taught the custom to their young and so forth.

The story of the "Hundredth Monkey" has often been used to show how social change takes place. It takes only one to be a change agent and create a chain reaction that brings about cultural change. The story also provides several lessons for those of us wishing to

113

improve relationships with our moms. First, if we don't want to keep eating the unpalatable "grit and grime" we are subject to in our mother-daughter associations, it's up to us to clean up the circumstances so we don't have to swallow so much muck.

Second, if we bring about this change, others may learn from us. Though our mothers may seem firmly established in set patterns, they may still be able to pick up new habits we can teach them. Our children, too, may develop healthier ways to interact and relate with us and in turn will pass these new ways of coping and interfacing along to their own children and so forth.

In the business world it's vital for corporations to stay abreast of current trends and methods of operation if they are going to stay on top. Those that don't change with the times go the way of the dinosaur and eventually experience devastating downturns in business or the unthinkable—closure.

Some companies bring in professional "change agents" or assign change teams to analyze what needs changing and to motivate employees to bring the desired results. In the last chapter we talked about inner change, recognizing that much of the change we want to see starts with our own internal change. In this chapter we'll look at action we can take and alterations we can make to bring about improvements in our relationship with our mother. Below are five elements that can bring about change in our mother-daughter relationships.[3]

1. **Desire.** We must sincerely want the change. Drawing closer to our mother will happen only if we are no longer happy living with the status quo and decide to make it happen.

2. **Objective.** We have to decide what we want to happen and determine what is necessary in order to reach that desired outcome.

3. **Motivation.** We have to implement the plan and stick with it in order to reach the envisioned goal.

4. **Collaboration.** We may need to work with others in order to make it happen. For instance, we may need a family member

or friend to team up with us, offer support, and stand as an accountability partner in order to see it through.

5. **Metamorphosis.** Our relationship will experience transformation if we put all the aforementioned into effect.

Carolyn was determined to cultivate a good relationship with her two teen daughters, but it wasn't easy. Like many other teens, they had erected walls that shut their mother out. "At first I was sorely tempted to 'accept the moat' separating me from my daughters. What kept me from doing that was God's command for me to be the primary influence in their lives."[4]

Carolyn understood how important it was to close the rift that had formed between her and her daughters. However, as most parents know, when kids reach the teenage years, the distance that separates parent and child can seem like a moat filled with ravenous alligators. Because Carolyn valued a close relationship with her daughters more than she feared navigating treacherous waters, she determined to do whatever she could to reach them. One of her solutions was to schedule regular outings with her girls during which she talked with them about what was going on in their lives.

The gap between you and your mother may also feel like a moat with the drawbridge up. Like Carolyn, you may need to take deliberate steps to close the distance between you. It won't happen by chance but rather by intentionally scheduling a rendezvous with your mom. The more often these gatherings happen, the more second nature scheduling them will become until they become a habit. There's no need to mention the reason for the meetings. Just let your mom know that spending more time with her is important to you. She'll be delighted you are.

BE PERSISTENT

Most people don't succeed the first time they try to erase old patterns, so don't be surprised if you find yourselves traveling the same rutted road. Henry Ford wrote, "If you're not succeeding at the level you'd like to succeed, my best advice to you is to double your rate of failure."

Change is never easy, and it rarely happens the first time around but only after a persistent, determined effort—and sometimes many failures. One of the reasons for meeting with your mother is to narrow the moat separating you. It has taken years to dig it as deep and wide as it is. Don't become discouraged by this seemingly impossible task.

Surely this is how Joshua must have felt when God assigned him the daunting job of leading an army into the walled city of Jericho in order to capture the city. (Read Joshua 5:13-6:27.) Our omnipotent God could have given him the city, but that would have done nothing to increase Joshua's or the Israelites' faith. Joshua must have quaked in his boots as he drew near the city walls. This was the same city Joshua had sent two spies to survey, and they were hidden from discovery by Rahab the prostitute (Joshua 2:2-7).

When Caleb and his group of spies returned from Cannan, their reports of what they had seen made the people tremble with fear. "We went into the land to which you sent us, and it does flow with milk and honey! Here is its fruit. But the people who live there are powerful, and the cities are fortified and very large. We even saw descendants of Anak there. The Amalekites live in the Negev; the Hittites, Jebusites and Amorites live in the hill country; and the Canaanites live near the sea and along the Jordan" (Numbers 13:27-29).

The men who had gone into the land were afraid of the fierce Nephilim, a race of men either so ferocious or large, or both, that it caused them to quake at the mere mention of them. These warriors were so daunting that the Israelites compared themselves to grasshoppers in their eyes (verses 31-33).

This was the land the Israelites had been promised by God and Moses but were never allowed to take possession of because of their disobedience. It was to this land that Joshua was leading the Israelites into battle. There seemed little hope of winning a battle against a race exhibiting such strength and power. As he neared the city, Joshua spied a man standing in front of him with a drawn sword. Unsure of who he was or what his intentions were, Joshua asked, "Are you for us or for our enemies?" (Joshua 5:13).

"Neither," he replied, "but as commander of the army of the LORD I have now come." Then Joshua fell facedown to the ground in reverence, and asked him, "What message does my Lord have for his servant?" The commander of the LORD's army replied, "Take off your sandals, for the place where you are standing is holy." And Joshua did so *(Joshua 5:14-15)*.

As God unfolded His plan to Joshua, it must have sounded ludicrous. God wanted him to send the priests before him blowing trumpets while Joshua and his men marched around the city seven times. So much for the element of surprise. In his heart, Joshua must have questioned God's judgment. (This is reminiscent of the seemingly irrational order God had given Abraham, ordering him to sacrifice his only son, Isaac.)

Each day Joshua, his men, and priests rallied together, marched around the city one time, and blew their trumpets. Can you imagine Joshua explaining the insanity of this plan to his men? "You want us to do what?" Surely the men must have questioned Joshua's judgment and the Lord's promise to give him the city.

On the seventh day Joshua went through this pattern one final time, ending the march with a great blast on the trumpets by the priests. All the people gave a shout, and the walls of Jericho came crashing down (Joshua 6:15-20).

The story of the destruction of the city of Jericho provides many lessons. First, God has a divine plan that to finite mortals often looks absurd. Second, if we do what God asks us to do, even when it makes little sense to us, He will honor us. Third, when we act in faith and are faithful to Him, our faith increases, and with it come rewards of a greater faith. Finally, we must be persistent in our faith even when we grow weary. Success might be just around the corner.

Relationships are like gardens—they need water to grow. You can't expect that your relationship with your mother will be strong unless you maintain it.[5]

The story of the battle of Jericho exemplifies the importance of faithfulness and persistence and is applicable to our strained relationships. It may take countless marches around a stronghold that is preventing healthy bonding. But if we are persistent in trying to break down the walls that divide us, they will eventually start to crumble.

In your own circumstances there are undoubtedly outcomes you want to see. What do you need to do in order to make them happen? It will take diligence and persistence to reach that goal.

BE VULNERABLE

Tight friendships develop in increments. People become friends by sharing pieces of their lives one small bit at a time until trust is built up to share greater things. In order to draw closer to our moms, we will also have to open our hearts. To many of us, it goes against our self-preservation instincts—like leaving the front door unlocked in a dangerous neighborhood. We run the risk of being misunderstood or hurt by the other person, and the thought of opening a new wound or rubbing salt into an old one makes us squirm.

In her book *Walking on Water* Madeleine L'Engle told the story of an English friend who was married to an officer in the Royal Air Force during World War II. She did the best she could to care for their three small children while he was away but worried daily about his welfare. One day he showed up at their London home unannounced. He explained he would soon be leaving for a dangerous mission and had been given permission by his superiors to stop over to visit his family. His wife wept tears of joy as she hugged his neck, and the children gathered around him.

She hadn't expected his visit, so there was little food in the house. She left the kids in his care and went to the market to shop for food in order to prepare a celebratory meal upon her return. While she was gone, her house was hit by a daylight bombing raid that leveled the home, killing her husband and all three of her children.

Madeleine's friend felt as if she, too, had died that day. Each day she forced herself to get out of bed. In order to move through her grief, she spent the rest of the war helping other war victims and rebuilding her life from the ashes. Eventually, she met and fell in love with a man who proposed marriage.

She was faced with a difficult decision. It seemed to her that marrying him would mean she had forgotten about the family she had lost. In the midst of such tragedy what right did she have for joy? The safest solution was to reject the offer and remain single. She would be safe and would not have to open herself up to such deep hurt and loss again. After much soul-searching, she chose to love, and she exchanged safety for marriage. She was willing to take a risk in the hope of living a full life again.[6]

Sometimes we are like Madeleine L'Engle's friend. We have lost so much and been hurt so much by the words and actions of those we love that we have locked our heart behind an iron door, fearing that if we unlock it, the pain will be more than we can bear. If we are not willing to make ourselves vulnerable, we won't have to feel the pain of the hurt. But we also won't experience the love that could be ours.

Henry Cloud describes the shell we build around ourselves as a psychological coat we don in order to prevent hurt. "God promises to give us new relationships in his family, but we have to work at taking off our coats in order to enjoy the newfound warmth."[7]

Jesus made himself vulnerable and suffered affliction for us in order that we might have a healthy and whole relationship with Him and His Father. "But he was pierced for our transgressions, he was crushed for our iniquities; the punishment that brought us peace was upon him, and by his wounds we are healed" (Isaiah 53:5).

Be willing to venture vulnerability, and make sacrifices in order to restore your relationship. It might mean opening up more and sharing with her. You might even share prayer requests with her or ask how you can pray for her. Start by talking about small matters. As you build trust, you can go deeper. Chances are that if you do, she will too. If she breaches your confidence, gently tell her how this hurts, and provide an example of what happened. Let her know you will not be able to share on a deeper level until she can keep your secrets and do so without judging.

TALK ABOUT THE HURTS

We've spent some time identifying our hurts, delving into the past, learning more about a mother's personality and her love languages. Hopefully, what you have learned has softened your heart toward your mother. It is never easy to talk about past wounds, especially when those who had a hand in causing them continue to cause them.

To cross over the moat, we must be willing to talk about some of the matters that created it in the first place. It's difficult to know how to begin. You might start by asking your mother if you can talk with her privately about something that has been troubling you. Since this can be an emotional time in which feelings are laid bare, you'll want to avoid public places for your meeting. Your mom's place or yours are both good choices.

Start by affirming all the great things she's done for you. You've already gotten a great start on this in one of the preceding chapters.

Once you have cushioned the conversation, you can talk about your feelings. Tell her what's on your heart, that you want a better relationship with her. Explain the hurts you have been feeling. This might either come as a complete surprise to her, or she may already be aware of the problem.

This is not the time to dump a truckload of wrongs on her. Choose a few of the most hurtful ones, recounting your memory of how they happened; then allow her to respond without condemning her.

It is easy to fall back into the old parent-child relationship with a parent. Now that you are grown, you are under God's authority, not your parents'. If you find yourself responding to your mother as you would have during childhood days, remind yourself of your adult status and that God, not your mother, is your source of authority.

Henry Cloud wrote, "We must take authority over what is delegated to us and redeem what has been lost, so we can give it back to him. We must take the role of authoritative ruler in the domains of our lives and follow his example in order to be agents of redemption. Then, we will reign forever with him as a joint heir."[8]

Paul wrote, "When I was a child, I talked like a child, I thought like a child, I reasoned like a child. When I became a man, I put childish ways behind me" (1 Corinthians 13:11). You are no longer a child who must submit but rather an adult with options. The key to healing is in your hands and God's. In order for it to happen, you must be willing to take a chance by talking about the past.

CONNECT AND COMMUNICATE

Connecting and communicating are two crucial ways bonds are built. Connecting has more to do with physically being present with your mother, while communicating is how you express your feelings to her and share information.

When communication isn't good between mother and daughter, we may become depressed, angry, and even emotionally distant. One way to improve communication is to look for ways to converse with her. This may mean calling her more often to talk about day-to-day happenings and asking her how she is doing.

In my relationship I may avoid talking with my mother, because the conversations are often one-sided. I merely listen. As a parent I learned that high-quantity time is as important as high-quality time. When we spend more time with a person, there is more opportunity for deep bonding. We'll have more frequent connection opportunities, which increase the likelihood of deeper bonding happening. If instead of making infrequent phone calls I check in more often, I'll also increase the chance of making better connections. One of my objectives for working toward improvement is to call my mother more often.

Even so, I may still be exasperated if I feel I'm not doing enough of the talking. So my next goal might be to learn to steer the conversation. In my case this won't happen without interrupting her, but once I do, I can direct the conversation to the topic I wish to speak on. Once I've had my "time" with her, I can redirect the conversation again, picking up the threads of what she was saying to show her that what she has to say matters too. I have personally done this in several previous conversations and find it works well. She does not see it as an offense. In fact, she hardly notices.

Some people are better at putting their feelings in writing rather than conversing on the phone. If this is you, consider sending your mom an occasional card or letter. I recommend you avoid doing this via e-mail, because it's easy to hit "send" before fully thinking things through. Once you hit "send," you cannot take the words back.

Scheduling more frequent rendezvous with our moms—for example, dinner out—is another possible solution. Additional ways I have found to connect include sharing photos with her of my kids and grandchild or photos of special events I've been involved in. I've never been into photos much, but I know they are important to my mom.

The younger generation, at least my children, nieces, and nephews, do not provide hard copies of photos. Instead, they send links to web sites where videos and photos can be viewed or downloaded. My mother, though computer literate, hates having to deal with this. She doesn't like this new method of sharing photos, though they are, in my opinion, easy to access and just a click away. Her attitude used to irritate me, because I saw it as laziness. She did not want to learn how to do this simple task.

I finally decided that although she is capable of retrieving these shots, the best solution for my peace of mind is to print copies of the photos for her. It's a happy trade-off, and I'm much happier when she is happy.

Most moms want to keep up with what is happening in their grandchildren's and great-grandchildren's lives. Be willing to share what is going on with your children and grandchildren with her.

CONSIDER THE NEXT GENERATION

Change agents not only consider necessary changes for the present but also alterations to improve the future. We may see only what changes can do for our relationship with our mother for the short term, when, in fact, whatever we alter now may affect our relationships with our children and their relationships with theirs. We can be the one hundredth monkey and hand it down. One of our objectives should be to work on developing close-knit relationships with our own daughters. The principles we apply to connecting with our mothers can be applied to connecting with our children.

Good relationships don't happen by chance but are the result of intentional cultivation. If we avoid communicating with our kids because it's either too much work or too stressful, they will probably use the same parenting techniques with their own children. If we are hands-on and very involved and communicative with our kids, they will most likely be the same way with theirs.

Parenting is the hardest job I've ever had. One has to persistently enforce rules, stay in touch with what is going on in his or her children's lives, and work hard to connect and communicate.

BE A FRIEND

"A man of many companions may come to ruin, but there is a friend who sticks closer than a brother" (Proverbs 18:24). This verse reminds us of the value of deep friendships. Having someone to share joys and triumphs with, to cling to in the storms of life, is a rare gift. God is this type of friend. When all other friends fall away,

He is there—a steady shoulder to lean on. If we abide with Him, He will abide with us. His friendship reflects the type of friendship we could have with our mother.

A relationship that mirrors even a fraction of the friendship God offers us requires sacrificial love on our part. It will take thick skin, willingness to forgive, deliberate acts of compassion, and persistent attempts to connect. We are the change agents who can make it happen, one small step at a time. Change can start with something as simple as doubling the amount of visits we pay to our mother and can grow into a time of actually looking forward to the visits. We can take the risk and perhaps fail, or do nothing and keep things the way they are. In the end, the decision to change or stay the same is up to us.

HEALING THOUGHTS

1. What can you do to create more connecting points with your mother? Be specific. _____

_____

_____

_____

2. What does the story of Joshua and his troops marching around Jericho teach us? _____

_____

_____

_____

3. What fears do you have about opening up and sharing with your mother? _____

_____

_____

_____

4. Which is more true and why? You act like a child when you interact with your mother, or you act like an adult. _____

_____

_____

_____

5. How can connecting and communicating help the next generation after us with their mother-daughter relationships?

_____

_____

_____

ELEVEN

SETTLING FOR "GOOD ENOUGH"

———— ◈ ————

It's admirable to strive for excellence but foolish to expect
perfection. Excellence pursues high standards but leaves
room for mistakes and even expects them.
—Sue Edwards and Kelly Mathews[1]

Despite the deep longing and sincere efforts to draw closer to those we love, sometimes we cannot have the close-knit relationship we long for. Psalm 68:6 speaks of this tension and gap between family members: "God sets the lonely in families, he leads forth the prisoners with singing; but the rebellious live in a sun-scorched land." The word "set" in this context means placed.

Psalm 68 speaks of God's faithfulness, dependability, and power over our enemies. The reference to families seems almost out of place in this psalm. What would have possessed David to write such a thing? I think David is addressing the feeling of isolation and loneliness we can experience even when we are a part of a family. Sometimes families become a place of desolation, even a battleground, when dysfunction threatens to destroy or ostracize us.

David had been chosen by God to replace Saul as king, and though this was God's appointment, it still came at a high cost. For several years David had to move from place to place, living in caves and fields as he tried to stay out of reach of King Saul's wrath and jealousy. Surely during this time he must have longed for the loving family and stable home he had left behind.

When David finally did assume the throne, he ruled with wisdom and authority. Despite his devotion to God, he didn't always make good choices. We see this when he misused his power and took beautiful Bathsheba, the wife of one of the officers in his army, to his bed (2 Samuel 11). It wasn't enough that he committed adultery—he then covered up the sin by sending Uriah, her husband, to the front lines to be killed. He couldn't hide what he did from God, and when the truth was revealed, David bitterly repented and pleaded for mercy. Though God forgave him, he still had to deal with the consequences.

Like a house built on a fault line, the crack began to spread until the family foundation began to crumble. The child Bathsheba bore David died (2 Samuel 12:15-19). Later, David's own son, Absalom, killed his brothers in an act of revenge against his brother, Amnon, for raping his sister Tamar (2 Samuel 13). Talk about a dysfunctional family!

Absalom was ostracized for what he did, and David longed to restore his relationship with his wayward son. But once again we see how beauty and power can be used for ill. Absalom was a very handsome and charismatic young man. He proceeded to manipulate and control those around him, building his political power in an attempt to wrest the kingdom from David's hands. Eventually it pitted David and his army against Absalom and his as Absalom attempted a coup against David's rule (2 Samuel 9-14).

David understood about the "lonely" in families and the pain of wanting to trust and love close friends and family members. He also saw that things did not always turn out the way one wished for.

It's interesting to note that verse six of Psalm 68 talks about God leading forth the prisoners with singing and that the rebellious live in a sun-scorched land. When we have made every attempt to remain close to our mother but she continues to hurt us, it can feel as if we are imprisoned. Her choices and ways of coping can make her life and the lives that overlap hers as unhappy and dry as a draught-stricken desert.

In Psalm 68:19 David also wrote, "Praise be to the Lord, to God our Savior, who daily bears our burdens." Despite the tough road he had traveled with friends and family, David still knew his true source of strength. In an earlier chapter I wrote about identifying with the trapped bird beating against a window in my relationship with my mother. I think David also identified with this feeling. At times family relationships can feel hopeless, yet David also recognized that God can carry the heavy weight such unhappiness can cause.

Like David, we must learn to rely on a higher source when we experience the "lonely" in our family relationships. We can control how we respond to someone but can do very little to control how he or she responds to us.

ACCEPTING THE INEVITABLE

Despite your attempts, restoration of your relationship may not happen. This can be true for several reasons:

You confront your mother and nothing changes. In the previous chapters we looked at change and how much of it depends on you. You can, in your attempts to bring change, talk with your mother and express your desire to improve the relationship, but there is no guarantee she will take what you have said to heart. There is also a possibility that she may misunderstand what you say or twist it and hold it against you. Sometimes people are not capable of understanding what you are trying to say or show.

She isn't a Christ-follower. If you follow Christ, you use His example and His teachings as your foundation, as well you should. But if your mother doesn't have a relationship with Christ, she doesn't operate from the same moral foundation. Her actions and thoughts are based on what seems right to her at the time. We should not be surprised, then, when she does not align with your way of thinking.

When someone you love rejects Christ, it can create deep grief in you, because it not only separates that person from God and the fulfilled life you know he or she is missing, but it separates the person from you because he or she doesn't understand or even want to hear the spiritual talk or references you make to Christ. You grieve, because your loved one does not have the joy and peace you know he or she could have.

Mark 13:12-13 quotes sobering words. Jesus was speaking of the end times as He told His disciples how it would be. "Brother will betray brother to death, and a father his child. Children will rebel against their parents and have them put to death. All men will hate you because of me, but he who stands firm to the end will be saved."

He wasn't so much trying to paint a bleak picture as He was preparing them to stand firm.

When even the people you love turn against you and ridicule you because of your faith, it is so much easier to relinquish beliefs in order to keep the peace. God wants us to hold fast to our faith. It is difficult to share the salvation story with people who know us well. Even Jesus, when He came to His hometown of Nazareth and proclaimed that He was the long-awaited Messiah, was ridiculed because people had seen Him grow up there—how could He possibly be the Son of God?

All spoke well of him and were amazed at the gracious words that came from his lips. "Isn't this Joseph's son?" they asked. Jesus said to them, "Surely you will quote this proverb to me: 'Physician, heal yourself! Do here in your hometown what we have heard that you did in Capernaum.' I tell you the truth," he continued, "no prophet is accepted in his hometown" *(Luke 4:22-24).*

If we want our mother to enter into a relationship with Christ, but she is not open to hearing it, it will do no good to keep hammering away at her. This is where we have to let go and let God do the rest. We may not be able to talk about our faith, but we can let it shine through, and we can also pray for her. There is a great quote I remember a friend sharing with me a long time ago that comes to mind time and again: "We may be the only Bible someone ever reads." Let your faith stand strong through your actions, and keep sending up prayers on your mother's behalf.

She cannot forgive, because she doesn't understand or doesn't want it. I have heard some daughters share heartbreak that has remained with them from their past. They may have been rebellious in their youth or have done or said something that caused a rift between them and their mother. Sometimes a mother cannot move past this. There is nothing we can do, other than pray, if our mother won't forgive a past wrong. We can, however, forgive her for her attitude.

Neither can we force her to become friends with us. Some mothers are so broken they don't realize they are missing a deep relationship. They may be content to stay where they are. Other mothers may not understand that their relationship is not what it could be.

Sara shared about how she and her mother currently coexist.

I'm coming to a place where I accept that my mother and I may never have a close relationship. We get along well and enjoy spending time together on the occasions that I am home to visit, but we aren't what you would call "close." We don't talk on the phone or correspond between my visits home. She has her life, her friends, her routine, and she's happy with them. It does still hurt my feelings at times when she chooses others ahead of me, but I also know that if I really needed her, she would come. Twice now, when I have been ill, she has dropped everything to come take care of me.

We have to accept the inevitable. Sometimes we have to learn to live with a "good-enough" relationship.

BOUNDARIES AND DISTANCE

We've talked a lot about accepting our mother right where she is, but sometimes relationships can be so destructive that if we let them go, they can destroy not only us but our family as well. Those with controlling mothers are particularly at risk. If you have made attempts to come to terms with your mom and she has a stranglehold on you, it may be time to set boundaries in order to stay spiritually, emotionally, and physically healthy.

One daughter whose mother was always criticizing and nagging her about her decisions pertaining to her children finally had had enough. She set firm rules for her mother's visit, informing her that criticizing how she raised her children was off limits. If her mother didn't comply, she would be given one warning that she would be taken home. If she did it again, they sent her packing. If the behavior kept up, she informed her mom that she would no longer be invited for visits to their home. This may seem harsh, but her mother's inability to let go was overlapping into her daughter's and her husband's authority.

I had to establish boundaries with my mother in my life and in my heart. Nowadays we communicate [by phone or by e-mail] only if there is serious illness or death within the family—once or twice a year at most. I've tried letting time pass and reconnecting, but the strain is so intense, I decided to just let it go (Tracy).

Henry Cloud says, "Many people struggle to discover, set, and guard their personal boundaries. They truly cannot tell where they end and someone else begins, and thus they suffer from lack of purpose, powerlessness, panic, identity loss, eating disorders, depression, irresponsibility, and a whole host of other problems, all which lead to a lack of real intimacy with others."[2]

If you are allowing you mother to manipulate you and rule your life, your marriage, or even your childrearing, then both you and she have boundary issues. Nothing will change unless you confront her and establish a line that cannot be crossed. By doing this, you will improve both her emotional health and your own.

Greg Baer writes, "If you want your life to change, you have to face up to what your mother's behavior means. Real love is caring about the happiness of another person without any concern for what we'll get in return. It's unconditional."[3]

Sometimes, despite attempts to improve the relationship, you simply cannot deal with all the baggage that comes with your mom's and your relationship. If it's threatening to pull you under or if it's causing a rift in your own family, it may be necessary to distance yourself. Some women have found peace by letting go. They make themselves less available to their mom, answer the phone less, try to have less contact with her. This should be the last resort, but sometimes it's necessary.

In extreme cases, daughters have moved farther away from their mother to make meddling less possible or minimize the effect of the mother's emotional instability or neediness. It's sad to think that creating physical distance is the answer, but in some cases it may be the only solution.

SETTLING FOR "GOOD ENOUGH"

I made up my mind that I would hang in there all the way in an effort to resolve conflicts that were present in my relationship with her. I do not believe I did the wrong thing, although I do regretfully admit that I didn't seem to know how to break out of the bickering mold that seemed to have a death grip upon my mom's and my relationship with each other—all the way through to the end of her life (Yvonne Joan Hill).

Years ago I remember reading an article by a young mother called "The Good Enough Mom." She talked about her quest to be the perfect mom and how exhausting it was. She wanted to be the mother who went to the PTA meetings, baked cookies for the class parties, sewed beautiful costumes for the school play, managed the soccer practice, created gourmet meals for her family, and kept the house spotless. However, she had finally realized that this was an unreachable goal. Instead of being the perfect mother, this young mom had determined that she would be a "good enough" mom by lowering her expectations.

Her house wasn't spotless, and she couldn't be in multiple places at the same time. Nevertheless, she was involved in her children's lives and doing a great job. Her decision to lower the bar had been very freeing. We may need to take our cues from this young mother and lower our expectations, settling for a "good enough" relationship with our mom. Bringing about radical change may not be possible.

At the beginning of this book I talked about our longing for the fairy tale-perfect mother and daughter relationship we may desire but cannot have. Remember the example of the photo of actress Gwyneth Paltrow and her mother, Blythe Danner? At some point we must stop beating against the window and accept our relationship for what it is. Once we do, we can experience relief and even peace that frees us to carry on without the pain and frustration we endure when we are determined to make it better.

Give your relationship back to God and, like the weary bird exhausted from its futile attempts to escape, rest in Him. Psalm 62:1 provides a wonderful visual example of the kind of rest we can have. "My soul finds rest in God alone; my salvation comes from him."

WHEN GOOD ENOUGH ISN'T GOOD ENOUGH

All of us struggle with elements of brokenness. However, occasionally people are so broken that they and those connected to them are caught in a pounding surf of ebbs and flows. Some women have found that a healthy connection with their mother isn't possible. In some cases a mother has mental illness that is either diagnosed or undiagnosed, so having a stable relationship isn't feasible. The ongoing drama and ups and downs of such an emotional attachment can eventually put your own mental health at risk.

Staying emotionally tied to someone broken in this way can create unbearable anguish. Some women fill their mother-daughter relationship void through fulfilling friendships with other women near their mother's age. One of the joys of being a part of the Body of Christ is the ties and support networks we enjoy through other Christians. In my own life, many moves have kept me from being in close proximity to family members much of the time, but I have found great friendships through church connections and small groups. Often the bonds that have been forged have been just as close as blood relationships. If it weren't for the care and nurture of some of these folks, I don't know how I would have managed.

Mothers and daughters can also find joy in being role models and mentors to other women such as are mentioned in Titus 2:3-5:

> Likewise, teach the older women to be reverent in the way they live, not to be slanderers or addicted to much wine, but to teach what is good. Then they can train the younger women to love their husbands and children, to be self-controlled and pure, to be busy at home, to be kind, and to be subject to their husbands, so that no one will malign the word of God.

What a joy to know those types of relationships are available to us because Christ serves as the common thread that ties us together!

On the whole, my mom was a good mom, regardless of our issues. But I work in ministry and have seen a lot of examples of mothers who really don't care for their children. For women with these types of mothers, I'd just like to say that God does set the lonely in families. Even though I am not very close to my own mother, I have been blessed to be surrounded by mothers. God has given me several wonderful, godly women who speak into my life on a regular basis. If one's own mother can't or won't be the mother that you need, God can provide a mother figure to walk through with you (Sarah).

GOD WILL HONOR YOUR EFFORTS

God desires restoration of relationships, but we must do our part to bring them about. If despite our best efforts they still don't happen, He will honor our efforts and provide opportunity for healthy relationships apart from our "blood" connection.

My mother is very determined, bull-headed, always right, can never be told anything, and if I want to have a relationship with her, I have to accept her as she is. Instead of resenting these character flaws, I recognize them as who she is and deal with them. So I back off. I can be right and not say it. I can be right and not correct her. I can know that I'm right and not have to hear her say it. I can accept more now and not have to change her into what I think she should be. She's taught me an invaluable lesson: relax and enjoy people the way they are. Celebrate them. And be comfortable enough with who I am that I don't always have to be right. Sometimes the need to be right keeps people from enjoying each other (Tamera).

Looking back, Yvonne muses—

I admit that sometimes I think I didn't do enough to get better acquainted with Mom while she was living. I think these things in retrospect since she passed away. But on the other hand, I believe I did as much as I was humanly able to on this earth, considering that I am a fallible human. Forgiveness must enter the picture in our relationships. We have to forgive our moms and other loved ones not only for what they've done but also for what they haven't done. We also need to forgive ourselves. Maybe, too, we should learn to relax on the subject of understanding and being understood and simply learn to accept and appreciate each other as we are. Stress the positives, and try to sweep the negatives under the rug. After we're finished mulling them over and hashing and rehashing them, they can be put to rest. Then we can go about living the rest of our life for the Lord.

God honors your good intentions. Do not be discouraged when your attempts to connect are rebuffed, ignored, or criticized. Proverbs 3:5-6 reminds us that God will be there for us, guiding our efforts, if we will only trust in Him. "Trust in the LORD with all your heart and lean not on your own understanding; in all your ways acknowledge him, and he will make your paths straight."

HEALING THOUGHTS

1. What do you think Psalm 68:6 means about God setting the lonely in families? _____

_____

_____

_____

2. What advice would you give to someone who is trying to improve a relationship with a family member who is not a Christ-follower? _____

_____

_____

_____

3. What do you think of the advice that we may have to settle for a "good enough" relationship? _____

_____

_____

_____

4. Is there anyone in your life who has been like a mother to you besides your mother? If yes, explain. _____

_____

_____

_____

5. What does Proverbs 3:5-6 mean by saying God will make your paths straight if you trust in Him? _____

_____

_____

_____

TWELVE

HOPE OF RESTORATION AND RENEWAL

———————◆———————

Extend a hand whether or not you know it shall be grasped.
—Ryunosuke Satoro[1]

Several years ago, Dorothy held a meeting with Anna, a company client. She wasn't her usual, peppy self, and Dorothy asked Anna if everything was all right. With tears in her eyes, she told Dorothy her mother had died a few weeks earlier. She had always been closer to her dad. They were alike in many ways with similar tastes and personalities that meshed beautifully.

Anna explained. "My mother and I were so different. I always felt that if one of my parents died, it would be my father's death that would impact me the most." However, her mother's death had left her reeling.

"Dorothy, I can't tell you how lost I felt and how very alone I was. One day, after leaving my office, an overwhelming despair washed over me. As I drove down the street, I hunted for the first church I could find. I pulled into the parking lot and went inside. I did something I had never done before—I prayed in this quiet, sacred spot, and it helped me feel better." She was pensive for a moment and then added, "When the person who carried me inside her body and gave me life died, I felt an emotional isolation I had never known before."

We are reminded by those who have lived longer than us that life is short, but until we grow older and experience the loss of a loved one, most of us don't realize the implications. The young adult child who fails to schedule regular visits to see her mother may believe she has all the time in the world, all the while unaware that her mother may be stricken with a serious illness a few years in the future.

Not one of us knows what tomorrow may bring. Though we may acquire cars, clothing, and property, our most precious possession is time. Dorothy's acquaintance did not realize this until it was too late. Even as you read this book, time is slipping away. Some of us who are older are more keenly aware of the passage of time than others, but it is happening nonetheless. If you don't attempt to make peace with your mother now, it may be too late a few years from now. Do what you can now to draw closer to her so you can live without regrets.

If after making attempts to do so you find your relationship cannot be improved, place it into God's hands. Though you want your mother to change, you cannot count on it. You must be the change you long to see. It begins with you. Through your relationship with Christ you are being renewed and transformed daily, and with that transformation comes a hope of renewed relationships.

"Therefore, we do not lose heart. Though outwardly we are wasting away, yet inwardly we are being renewed day by day" (2 Corinthians 4:16). Be encouraged. Though the years are fleeting and outward circumstances seem to be deteriorating, God assures us that inwardly we are being revitalized.

I went through a troubled mother-daughter relationship with my mother for many years. She just passed away one year ago at the age of ninety-eight. It wasn't until she went into a nursing home and began to lose her memory that she became the loving mother I wish she had been throughout the years. I was her only living child, and as I saw her become weak and feeble, my love and compassion for her grew (Margaret).

With time and perspective I was able to appreciate the good things she had done in my life. To this day she encourages all of us kids to follow our dreams. She bought me art supplies when I discovered I had artistic talent back when we had very little money. She took me to the library every week when I was growing up to nurture in me culture and hope. She brought me to museums and theater and orchestra concerts so that I would know that life held more than poverty and futility. She showed me a great example of Christian faith, attending church and faithfully supporting missions on next to nothing. I owe her so much. I can honestly say she is a great blessing and that I love her (Kathleen).

True transformation happens from the inside out.

GROWING TO MATURITY

I mentioned earlier that I work for a women's rescue mission that includes a day shelter and residential facility. The needs are great, and the brokenness at times is nearly unbearable. It is difficult not to become overly attached to these women. Sometimes one particular person touches your heart strings, and you want to give her extra assistance and grace. Our staff has learned the hard way that the worst thing they can do for these needy women is to keep bailing them out of the messes they have made. Doing so provides only a short-term solution and rarely ever helps for the long term.

The more we model our behavior to be like Christ's, the more like Him we become and the healthier our relationships grow. Christ understood that there is a healthy kind of love and a distorted kind, and He responded to people's needs like a stern but loving parent. He both challenged and loved people according to their spiritual and physical standing and needs.

Paul in his letter to the Thessalonian church also took a parental approach. He compared his ministry to the church to the way a mother cares for her children: "As apostles of Christ we could have been a burden to you, but we were gentle among you, like a mother caring for her little children. We loved you so much that we were delighted to share with you not only the gospel of God but our lives as well, because you had become so dear to us" (1 Thessalonians 2:6-8).

The love of our Heavenly Father exemplifies the gentle, protective compassion of a mother's love. In real life, sometimes mother-daughter bonds become stretched and misshapen when what a mother or daughter believe to be love transforms into something manipulative or needy. One of a parent's roles is to move his or her child to maturity, nurturing the child to make wise decisions and become independent.

Move from childhood to adulthood in your mother-daughter relationship. Take a moment to gauge your "adult" relationship with your mother. Are you responding to her as an adult, or are you still reacting to her as if you were a child? Is she still running your life? Are you letting her? If so, it's time for you to break free of those unhealthy bonds. It won't be easy, but it is very crucial in order to establish a wholesome connection with her.

Cut the apron strings with your own children. How are you doing with your own adult children? Do you recognize their right to manage their own lives, households, and families, or are you attempting to manage them for them? If you continually give advice on decisions and lifestyle, you have not fully broken away from your dependent status. It's time, for the sake of your children, that you did.

It is one thing for your children to come to you to seek advice upon occasion, but if that frequently happens, you may need to let them make their own decisions. True, their choices may not always be wise, but those decisions are theirs to make nonetheless. Margaret Johnson, author of *18: No Time to Waste*, a book about her relationship with her eighteen-year-old daughter, noted, "I spoke for years after the book was published telling our story, and I came to realize that most mothers have difficulty letting go of their adult children. I was as honest as possible in writing the book and received hundreds of letters from teenagers and mothers telling of similar circumstances in their families."

Breaking free of control is imperative if you are going to move toward healthy bonds with your mother. As you work to mend the tears in the fabric that holds you together, consider the preciousness of your moments together.

CREATE MEMORIES

Sometimes we get so hung up on the hurts that we forget about the happy times. Don't forget to recall the good moments you've had with your mom. Motherhood is an amazing ride—a mixture of delightful firsts: first steps, first day of school, first date, tumbled together with anxious moments.

I'll never forget several times when I was a child waking in the middle of the night, ill from some virus—my mother, roused from a sound sleep, tenderly feeling my forehead or stroking my back as I leaned over a trashcan and unceremoniously lost my dinner. Surely she was weary and tired and wanted to do anything but listen to a sick child whimper, but she did it anyway. My mother always made sure there was a hot meal on the table every night so we could eat together as a family. Though she wasn't the tidiest housekeeper, she cleaned the house every Saturday like clockwork. Money was tight, but she saw to it that we had new clothes and shoes on occasion. I remember how hard she worked, packing suitcases and ice chests in preparation for our family's yearly vacation.

Mom never said, "I love you" in words, but she certainly said it in deeds, helping care for and coddle our menagerie of pets: dogs, hamsters, guinea pigs, gerbils, turtles, rabbits—even a pony. She let us play "tent" under the desk in the living room and saved large appliance boxes so we could make playhouses from them. Mom sewed homemade clothes, made and decorated birthday cakes, and soothed bee stings with baking soda. All along the way when we thought little of it, she left loving markers along my life journey that spoke of her affection for me.

Until we reflect on what our mothers have done for us, we don't realize their sacrifices. Now is the time to build memories. If the good times are scarce, you may be able to build better ones in the future.

An article on mother-daughter relationships suggests ways to commemorate the good experiences mothers and daughters have shared.

You need to create mementos and markers. Memories fade. That's why photo albums, scrapbooks, and creative memory notebooks are so important. Handprints in concrete, purity rings, marks inside closet doors with heights and dates, junk boxes with old trophies, patches, and certificates all create clutter but provide memories.[2]

While you still have your mother with you, take photographs of her. If possible, include yourself and your family members in them. Take time to thank her for what she has done for you. Look for activities that can help you build memories now. It might mean taking a craft class together, going out to a movie, taking slow walks together, redecorating a room, working on a flower garden, throwing a cookout for some of her friends.

The moments you give each other should be more about time spent together than about buying things for each other. As my husband likes to say, when people look back on their lives, they scarcely remember the expensive car they owned or trip they took. What they treasure most are the people they spent precious moments with and the love they shared.

Moms, the same can be said for making memories with your daughters. The common denominators may seem scarce, but they are there if you look for them. Make time for mother-daughter activities, even if it's hard to work them in. For a while my middle daughter, Gaby, and I were at odds as she went through the rebellious teenage years. It was a period in our lives neither of us would care to repeat, and Gaby has since come back and apologized for the grief she caused.

One week we had a "skirmish" just before we were scheduled to go for a mother-daughter date at a local ceramic shop. Both of us were clinging to the tie that bound us together as a drowning woman clings to a life preserver. We knew that the planned events were important in order to maintain the raveling thread. As we climbed into the car to make the short trip to the shop, the tension was nearly palpable.

During our time at the shop, however, the differences faded, and we worked side by side painting our fanciful mugs. The conversation wasn't deep. We talked about trivial things, but that time was a bridge-builder for us, and it remains a pleasant moment indelibly etched in our memories.

To forge strong connections one has not simply to find time but also to make time and spend time with the other person. The hearts of those who have learned to do this remain tied together as the years pass.

NOTHING BROKEN; NOTHING MISSING

Many of us are familiar with the Hebrew word *shalom*. In English it translates to "peace." Our language cannot fully capture the width and depth of the word's meaning. In Jesus' day when someone wished another person *shalom*, what he or she was actually wishing the person was wholeness—nothing broken and nothing missing.

This is what God wants for our lives and our relationships, not perfection but a wholeness of mind, body, and emotions and peaceful coexistence with others. He honors our efforts to bring this health and wholeness to our relationships.

Hebrews 12:14-15 reminds us, "Make every effort to live in peace with all men and to be holy; without holiness no one will see the Lord. See to it that no one misses the grace of God and that no bitter root grows up to cause trouble and defile many."

What does it meant to "see to it that no one misses the grace of God"? We are Christ's ambassadors, and as Christ's followers we are to extend His grace to others, especially the hard to love.

Cindi had never had a good relationship with her mom, but after becoming a Christian she realized the importance of putting her differences behind her. She was determined to make a fresh start with her mother:

I grew up in a family that fed off negativity. Conversation was based on tearing someone down instead of building them up. I learned at an early age that something was wrong with me, because I couldn't do anything that made anyone happy. As a matter of fact, I couldn't do anything right. That, of course, was not true, but I believed it to be so, and in my mind it was.

As a result of my parents' divorce, I started acting out in ways that showed my irresponsibility. I know now that I was searching for someone to comfort me, and when I didn't find that in the adults around me, I turned to drugs and sex to numb my pain. I gave my mom a really hard time during my teen years.

After Cindi made the decision to follow Christ, God began transforming her, but she still found it impossible to please her mother.

She nagged me about all of my choices, whether good or bad, if I didn't do things her way. I was just that rebellious.

Cindi joined a twelve-step program that revealed a lot about the baggage she carried. As she worked her way through it, she realized that she had become her mother.

Suddenly I understood her craziness. My father had hurt me worse than my mother ever did, but I didn't want to spend any time with my mom because of her nagging and inability to let me be me.

While working my fourth step on my resentment toward my father and being able to forgive him, I found forgiveness for my mom also. I realized that since my father had been dead for twenty years, my resentment toward him was only hurting me. So I was able to give that same forgiveness to my mother. When I realized that my parents had parents and that they had learned from their environment, I could see how they had developed their behaviors. Once I realized that, I knew I couldn't change that. I live by the Serenity Prayer: *God, grant me the serenity to accept the things I cannot change, courage to change the things I can, and the wisdom to know the difference.*

I cannot change my mom's behavior, but I can change my reactions. The wisdom to know the difference is that I accept my mom where she is and realize it's not a reflection on me. I'm doing the best I can with what I have to work with, and so is she. I choose not to allow my bitterness to keep me from spending time with her, because I have only a short time left with her. I've prayed and asked God to allow me to see my mother through His eyes and to feel toward her with His heart, because my heart is incapable of what His heart is capable of, and His eyes can see what mine can't see.

Now when she complains and grumbles or tries to manage my life, I just acknowledge her concern and don't worry about changing her or making her see things my way. I think my acceptance of her just as she is has freed me to be who I am and allows her to have her opinions. But ultimately God filled me with His love for her and allows me to see her through His eyes.

The Bible contains a story that teaches us about bitterness. When the Israelites came to Marah, they couldn't drink the waters because they were bitter. Moses, acting under God's direction, placed a tree in the waters so that the waters turned sweet and became drinkable (Exodus 15:23-25). Just as in the story of the Israelites, bitterness can ruin sweet waters. The differences between you and your mother can cause hostility and resentment to spread like a cancer. Cindi learned that she didn't have the power to change her past, but she did have the power to prevent bitterness caused by it.

When we allow God to work through us, we can see healing. Like Cindi, we can allow Him to make the waters sweet again.

STRENGTHENING THE TIES TO HIM STRENGTHENS THE TIES TO HER

Using God's words as your foundation, talking and listening to Him about your relationships, praying for your mother and for an improved attitude regarding how to respond to her—all are part of implementing change.

With God's help, I try to balance honesty with acceptance and love. This is definitely not something I do easily. But the greatest blessing has been that I've seen my mother growing kinder and more loving. I would like to take the credit for that, but it was all God's idea (Leslie).

Most people are transformed in small increments rather than instantaneously. Cara says, "Pray about it, and ask God to transition your relationship to a new level. Our moms are a wonderful resource if we're willing to accept them as they are. Also allow them to have flaws and not be perfect."

Here are some more thoughts from author Margaret Johnson:

My advice from this vantage point is to accept your mother just the way she is and to lovingly express your own feelings. She may or may not understand, but knowing the history of her parents and how they treated her may help you. I regret many things I said to my mother and wish I'd been more understanding. I take it as a lesson on how to treat my daughter and sons, and though I often fail, I am at least aware that they are independent adults and I must respect and treat them as such.

Laura suggests, "Reach out to your mom on your own level. Spend time with her, get to know her and her interests. Chances are that you will discover an amazing woman."

Many of the women mentioned in this book have found the secret to having a closer connection with their mothers. By allowing God to work on refining them, they have taken on His nature and have learned to respond to relationships in healthier ways. The connection women share with their mothers may never be the ideal they dreamed of, but it can become better.

Letting God serve as intermediary will help you suffer fewer wounds, forgive more freely, and love more deeply. Like a trapped bird, you can find your way to the open window and soar toward freedom.

HEALING THOUGHTS

1. What legacy will you leave your own children? _____

_____

_____

_____

_____

2. What legacy has your mom left for you? _____

_____

_____

_____

3. What can you do to build better memories between you and your mother? _____

_____

_____

_____

4. Name one thing you can do in your own mother-daughter relationship to make the waters sweet again. _____

_____

_____

_____

5. What Scripture reference mentioned in this book has been most helpful or comforting to you regarding your own mother-daughter relationship? Why? _____

_____

_____

APPENDIX

ENNEAGRAM OF PERSONALITIES

Below are the nine personality types. As you look them over, see if you can determine the one that most clearly defines you. You may be a blend of several. If after reviewing them you are still not sure about your personality type, ask some of your friends or family members to decide what descriptions identify you best.

Each personality type has its strengths and weakness.

Type One: The Reformer

The principled, idealistic type. Type Ones are conscientious and ethical with a strong sense of right and wrong. They are teachers, crusaders, and advocates for change, always striving to improve things but afraid of making a mistake. Well-organized, orderly, and fastidious, they try to maintain high standards but can slip into being critical and perfectionistic. They typically have problems with resentment and impatience. *At their best*: wise, discerning, realistic, and noble, they can be morally heroic.

Type Two: The Helper

The caring, interpersonal type. Type Twos are empathetic, sincere, and warmhearted. They are friendly, generous, and self-sacrificing but can also be sentimental, flattering, and people-pleasing. They are well-meaning and driven to be close to others but can slip into doing things for others in order to be needed. They typically have problems with possessiveness and with acknowledging their own needs. *At their best:* unselfish and altruistic, they have unconditional love for others.

Type Three: The Achiever

The adaptable, success-oriented type. Type Threes are self-assured, attractive, and charming. Ambitious, competent, and energetic, they can also be status-conscious and highly driven for advancement. They are diplomatic and poised but can also be overly concerned with their image and what others think of them. They typically have problems with workaholism and competitiveness. *At their best:* self-accepting, authentic, everything they seem to be—role models who inspire others.

Type Four: The Individualist

The introspective, romantic type. Type Fours are self-aware, sensitive, and reserved. They are emotionally honest, creative, and personal but can also be moody and self-conscious. Withholding themselves from others due to feeling vulnerable and defective, they can also feel disdainful and exempt from ordinary ways of living. They typically have problems with melancholy, self-indulgence, and self-pity. *At their best:* inspired and highly creative, they are able to renew themselves and transform their experiences.

Type Five: The Investigator

The perceptive, cerebral type. Type Fives are alert, insightful, and curious. They are able to concentrate and focus on developing complex ideas and skills. Independent, innovative, and inventive, they can also become preoccupied with their thoughts and imaginary constructs. They become detached yet high-strung and intense. They typically have problems with eccentricity, nihilism, and isolation. *At their best:* visionary pioneers, often ahead of their time, they are able to see the world in an entirely new way.

Type Six: The Loyalist

The committed, security-oriented type. Sixes are reliable, hard-working, responsible, and trustworthy. Excellent "trouble-shooters," they foresee problems and foster cooperation but can also become defensive, evasive, and anxious—running on stress while complaining about it. They can be cautious and indecisive but also reactive, defiant, and rebellious. They typically have problems with self-doubt and suspicion. *At their best:* internally stable and self-reliant, they courageously champion themselves and others.

Type Seven: The Enthusiast

The busy, productive type. Type Sevens are extroverted, optimistic, versatile, and spontaneous. Playful, high-spirited, and practical, they can also misapply their many talents, becoming over-extended, scattered, and undisciplined. They constantly seek new and exciting experiences but can become distracted and exhausted by staying on the go. They typically have problems with impatience and impulsiveness. *At their best:* they focus their talents on worthwhile goals, becoming appreciative, joyous, and satisfied.

Type Eight: The Challenger

The powerful, aggressive type. Type Eights are self-confident, strong, and assertive. Protective, resourceful, straight-talking, and decisive, they can also be ego-centric and domineering. Eights feel they must control their environment, especially people, sometimes becoming confrontational and intimidating. Eights typically have problems with their tempers and with allowing themselves to be vulnerable. *At their best:* self-mastering, they use their strength to improve others' lives, becoming heroic, magnanimous, and inspiring.

Type Nine: The Peacemaker

The easy-going, self-effacing type. Type Nines are accepting, trusting, and stable. They are usually grounded, supportive, and often creative but can also be too willing to go along with others to keep the peace. They want everything to go smoothly and be without conflict, but they can also tend to be complacent and emotionally distant, simplifying problems and ignoring anything upsetting. They typically have problems with inertia and stubbornness. At their best: indomitable and all-embracing, they are able to bring people together and heal conflicts.

NOTES

Prologue

1. Elizabeth Stone, *Mothers of the Bible Speak to Mothers of Today* (Birmingham, Ala.: New Hope, 2009), 125.

Chapter 1

1. *Miss Potter*, motion picture, directed by Chris Noonan (New York: Weinstein Company, 2007).

Chapter 2

1. William Paul Young, *The Shack* (Newbury Park, Calif.: Windblown Media, 2007), 154.

2. Jeff A. Benner (January 23, 2009), "Ancient Hebrew Thought," Ancient Hebrew Research Center, 1999-2007, <http://www.ancient-hebrew.org/12_thought.html>.

3. Wiki.answers.com (January 23, 2009), "What Is the Hebrew Translation of the Word *Mother*?" <http://wiki.answers.com/Q/What_is_the_Hebrew_translation_of_the_word_mother>.

4. Benner, "Ancient Hebrew Thought."

5. Dailyreader.net (January 27, 2009), "*Little Women*, by Louisa May Alcott," <http://www.dailyreader.net/content/read/Little-Women/3660?p=3>.

6. Mattias Thompson (April 20, 2011), *Autumn Sonata*, 1978, Internet Movie Data Base, <http://www.imdb.com/title/tt0077711>.

7. Paul Skery (April 20, 2011), *Mermaids*, 1990, Internet Movie Data Base, <http://www.imdb.com/title/tt0100140>.

8. Geoffrey A. Middleton (April 20, 2011), *Mommie Dearest*, 1981, Internet Movie Data Base, <http://www.imdb.com/title/tt0082766>.

9. Anonymous (April 20, 2011), *Because I Said So*, 2007, Internet Movie Data Base, <http://www.imdb.com/title/tt0490084>.

10. Stephanie Whitson, *Unbridled Dreams* (Ada, Mich.: Bethany House, 2008).

11. Denis McGregor, *Mama Drama: Making Peace with the One Woman Who Can Push Your Buttons, Make You Cry, and Drive You Crazy* (New York: St. Martin's Griffin, 1999).

12. Michael J. Fox (March 31, 2009), "Michael J. Fox (1961-)," The Quotations Page, <http://www.quotationspage.com/quotes/Michael_J._Fox/>.

13. Sue Edwards and Kelly Matthews, *Leading Women Who Wound* (Chicago: Moody Press, 2009), 52.

Chapter 3

1. Dinah Maria Mulock Craik (March 31, 2009), "Friends," Quoteland.com, <http://www.quoteland.com/topic.asp?CATEGORY_ID=63>.

2. *Ice Princess*, motion picture (Burbank, Calif.: Walt Disney Pictures, 2005).

3. Wikipedia.org (April 8, 2009), "Body Language," <http://en.wikipedia.org/wiki/Body_language>.

Chapter 4

1. Latest Dud (April 8, 2009), "How to Deal with a Controlling Mother," HubPages, <http://hubpages.com/hub/How-To-Deal-With-A-Controlling-Mother>.

2. (April 9, 2009), "The Max-Neff Model of Human Scale Development," Celebrate Empathy for Life, <http://www.celebrateempathy.com/Max-Neef.pdf>.

Chapter 5

1. Henry Wadsworth Longfellow (April 4, 2009), "History," Quoteland.com, <http://www.quoteland.com/search.asp>.

2. Dear Abby, "Wounded in California," *Hickory Daily Record*, January 12, 2009.

3. Enneagram Institute World Headquarters (January 9, 2009), "Type Descriptions," 1998-2008, <http://www.enneagraminstitute.com/descript.asp>.

4. Gary Chapman (January 9, 2009), "Learn the Languages: The Five Love Languages," Fivelovelanguages.com, <http://www.fivelovelanguages.com/learn.html>. Used with permission.

Chapter 6

1. Peter Drucker (April 22, 2009), "Communication," Quoteland.com, <http://www.quoteland.com/search.asp>.

2. Quoted in Edwards and Mathews, *Leading Women Who Wound: Strategies*, 99.

3. Quoted in Ibid.

Chapter 7

1. William Butler Yeats (June 2, 2009), Thinkexist.com, <http://thinkexist.com/quotation/what_do_you_think_of_when_alone_at_night-do_not/330132.html>.

2. Jack McGinnis and Barabara Shlemon Ryan, *The Truth Shall Set You Free: A Spiritual Program for People Recovering from Codependency and Life's Losses* (West Melbourne, Fla.: Be-Loved Ministry, 1991), 75.

Chapter 8

1. Paule Boese (June 3, 2009), "Quotes About Forgiveness," Quotegarden. com, <http://www.quotegarden.com/forgiveness.html>.

2. (January 5, 2009), "Forgiving the Unforgivable," Catholic Education Resource Center, <http://www.catholiceducation.org/articles/catholic_stories/cs0025.html>.

Chapter 9

1. (May 6, 2009), "Quotations About Daughters," Jewish proverb, Quote garden.com, <http://www.quotegarden.com/daughters.html>.

2. Cecil Murphy (January 12, 2008), "Who Says We Can't Change People?" in *The Man Behind the Words*, <http://hosted.verticalresponse.com/366575/8ef2784848/1502500157/819a584a1e/>.

3. Abraham Lincoln (January 12, 2008), "The Quotations Page," Quotation 31097, <http://www.quotationspage.com/quote/31097.html>.

4. *What About Bob?* motion picture (Burbank, Calif.: Touchstone Pictures, 1991).

5. Cross Map Dictionary (May 7, 2009), "talent," <http://dictionary.cross map.com/definition/talent.htm>.

6. Henry Cloud, *Changes That Heal* (Grand Rapids: Zondervan Publishing House, 1992) 37.

Chapter 10

1. Goethe (May 11, 2009), "Friendship Quotes: General," The Friendship Page, <http://www.friendship.com.au/quotes/quofri.html>.

2. Ken Keys Jr. (May 12, 2009), "The 100th Monkey," Wowzone.com, <http://www.wowzone.com/monkey.htm>.

3. Kirsten van den Hul (May 11, 2009), "A Change Agent?" Kirstenvan denhul.wordpress.com, <http://kirstenvandenhul.wordpress.com/2009/04/26/a-change-agent/>.

4. Carolyn Mahaney (May 11, 2009), "Building a Strong Mother-Daughter Friendship," Crosswalk.com, <http://www.crosswalk.com/1363344/>.

5. Marie Hughes (May 11, 2009), "How to Improve Your Relationship with Your Mother," Esortment.com, <http://www.essortment.com/lifestyle/improveyourrel_sczl.htm>.

6. Madeleine L'Engle, *Walking on Water* (Colorado Springs: Shaw/WaterBrook, 2001), 233-34.

7. Cloud, *Changes That Heal*, 84.

8. Ibid., 281.

Chapter 11

1. Edwards and Mathews, *Leading Women Who Wound*, 52.
2. Cloud, *Changes That Heal*, 107.
3. Greg Baer (May 17, 2009), "Controlling Mothers: Cutting the Apron Strings," Ezine Articles, <http://ezinearticles.com/?Controlling-Mothers: -Cutting-the-Apron-Strings&id=385159>.

Chapter 12

1. Ryunosuke Satoro Quotes (August 10, 2009), Brainy Quote, <http:// www.brainyquote.com/quotes/quotes/r/ryunosukes167567.html>.
2. Roseanne Rosen (May 8, 2009), "Repairing the Mother-Daughter Relationship," excerpt from *The Complete Idiot's Guide to Mothers*, 2001, <http:// life.familyeducation.com/girls/mothers/54568.html>.

SELECTED BIBLIOGRAPHY

Enneagram of Personality Theory (April 22, 2009), Buzzle.com, <http://www.buzzle.com/articles/enneagram-of-personality-theory.html>.

Free RHETI Sampler (August 11, 2009), <http://www.enneagraminstitute.com/dis_sample_36.asp>.

Hot Celebrity Photos (August 10, 2009), <http://hotcelebrity.name/wp-content/uploads/2009/01/313437161_39b7ad61d2_o.jpg>.

The Enneagram Institute World Headquarters, The home site of Don Richard Riso and Russ Hudson, copyright 1998-2007 (August 12, 2009), <http://www.enneagraminstitute.com>.

RECOMMENDED RESOURCES

Don Richard Riso, *Enneagram Transformations* (Boston: Mariner Books, January 29, 1993).

The Riso-Hudson Enneagram Type Indicator personality test (August 11, 2009), <http://www.enneagraminstitute.com/Tests_Battery.asp>.

Russ Hudson and Don Richard Riso, *Discovering Your Personality Type: The Essential Introduction to the Enneagram* (Boston: Mariner Books, 2003).